Reflections

Reflections

Ravi Batra

PARTRIDGE
A Penguin Random House Company

To order additional copies of this book, contact
Partridge India
000 800 10062 62
orders.india@partridgepublishing.com

www.partridgepublishing.com/india

ACKNOWLEDGEMENTS

1. *I am grateful to my parents and wife without whose encouragement, it would not have been possible.*

2. *I am indebted to his Excellency shri Loknath Misra'; Honourable Governor of Assam, His Excellency shri M.V. Dighe; Honourable Governor of Meghalaya & Vice Admiral Inderjit Bedi, AVSM; Commandant National Defence Academy who have given me their most valuable time and encouraged me through their most benign forewords.*

PREFACE

Dear Readers,

Encouraged by your warm response to my first effort 'Leadership in its Finest Mould'- Guru Govind Singh, I've endeavored again. 'Reflections' are my own thoughts and images. I know some critics will not find poems in conformity with traditional and orthodox style of English poetry. To my mind, that leaves a lot of scope for deviation between what the poet intends to communicate and what readers interpret, intrigued with their own sense of comprehension.

I've ventured to express own rhythms coined in simple and unambiguous words in rhymes. Readers gifted with pronounced aesthetic sense of modern western music, would appreciate that most of these well match the sounds of their instrument.

My effort had been, all throughout, to establish what we're doing and what we should be doing by candid expression of various truths of our lives, which, we knowingly, are shy of recognition and acceptance.

Your comments are most welcome and in-fact, I would consider them a source of inspiration.

-**Col Ravi Batra**

FOREWORD

Reading Col. Ravi Batra's book titled 'Reflections' was an immense pleasure and thought provoking. Gentle rhythm in the poems and a lucid & tasteful expression on themes which are undoubtedly laudable is soothing and rejuvenates one in one's otherwise busy & tension ridden life. It was heartening to note that person from profession of arms could devote his time so usefully and in such a healthy manner.

I congratulate Col. Ravi Batra for his commendable effort and recommend the book for pleasure reading for one and all especially our young generation who I am sure, can derive a lot of benefit for their practical day to day life & face challenges ahead.

8.10.91

Loknath Misra (Rajbhavan Guwhati)

F O R E W O R D

I have gone through Col. Ravi Batra's collection of poems : 'Reflections' with great delight and avid interest. The poet's sense of commitment to the readers as 'friend, philosopher and guide' has found its pristine expression in each line of the poems in impeccable style and chaste manner. Subjects addressed cover vast tapestry.

I congratulate the poet for his creditable attempt in the field of poetry. I hope the collection shall be a fit thought provoking and pleasure reading for all sections of readers from scholars to students and lay readers.

I wish the poet all success.

M.V. Diebe
Governor

वाइस एडमिरल इन्द्रजीत बेदी, ए वी एस एम
कमांडेन्ट
Vice Admiral Inderjit Bedi. AVSM
Commandant
Tele : 331700/6600 (O) 338898 (O)
6601 (R) 333600 (R)

राष्ट्रीय रक्षा अकादमी
एन डी ए खड़कवासला
पुणे – 411 023
National Defence Academy
PO NDA Khadakwasla
Pune – 411 023.

28 Nov 92

F O R E W O R D

1.   It has been a matter of considerable joy for
me to have become acquainted with Colonel Ravi Batra
during his current assignment as a Battalion
Commander of one of the Cadets' Battalions at the
Academy.   I had been pleasantly surprised to have
been made aware of his talent as a poet even before
he had joined the Academy and it is most heartening
to know that he is publishing his collection of
poems "Reflections".

2.   The poet in him aims at expressing his feelings
on a very wide variety of subjects offering
practical advice through his simple words written
in a rhythmic style.   His literary contribution and
the poetic talent deserves the fullest recognition.

3.   I congratulate Colonel Ravi Batra for this most
effective utilisation of his leisure hours.   I wish
him every success in his joyful efforts in giving
his readers many moments of reflection.

(Inderjit Bedi)
Vice Admiral
Commandant

Contents

REALISM

PRAGMATISM

COCKTAILS

DEDICATED
TO

Loving memory of my father
whose spark of sublime humanism
humility and humor in me
is
my only wealth.

-Ravi Batra

PATRIOTISM

PATRIOTISM

INDIA - THE UNMATCHABLE

My Country is as great as she could be.
Her history, culture and great heritage
    sans any parallel.
Her natural beauty, serenity in her lap is
    indeed unmatchable.
Her mountains throw unique challenge to
    man's indomitable will.
Flower laden valleys, snow-capped peaks,
misty dewy mornings infuse life even in still.
Her rivers dancing down the mountains seem
    to play hide and seek
Fascinating hot spring amidst snow,
    invite a spontaneous shriek.
Magnificent and bewitching beauty of
    Himalayas is par excellence.
Her woods are deep, dark and unusually dense.
    Her deserts hold anyone in bewilderment.
Great seas wash her shores as if, in
    reverential endowment.
A great variety of flowers make her
    air fragrant and reverberating.
Songs of colorful birds of all sorts keep
    life on her pulsating.
Wild life on her is real wild.
Her natural beauty coupled with ecological charm
    makes her look like a beautiful innocent child.
Whistling winds of her valleys, singing brooks
and majestic water falls in symphony with
songs of birds and bees, produce such an
    alluring ecological jazz.

All kinds of climates, you name any, she has.
Whole country is dotted with holy relics & shrines.
Her morning air due to chanting of holy scriptures &
hymns is unusually calm & sublime.
Monsoons bathe her from head to toe.
Blue waters of Indian ocean kiss her feet,
 as if, with an humble bow.
Her paintings, carvings and sculpture are
living symbols of universal truth, sobriety,
 unity of mankind and virtue of patience.
Her architectural monuments beat realms of imagination.
Her forts are living symbols of valour, unflinching
resolve and glorious martial traditions.
Her mountain ranges, worth thousands of expeditions.
Her classical music is a unique creation
 which, soothes both body and soul.
Over the cultural unity and spirit of India
 in its diversity, many a head roll.
A vivid story of her culture is enshrined in
 her alluring folk-lore.
Both are inseparable like a lion form his roar.
It is a fallacy to see India with her
 boundaries, as you see today, on a political map.
Remember, this great country in her glorious
past, had seven great seas in her lap.
With the rise and fall of civilizations and empires over her, she
had been very badly mauled.
One fourth of her original size only, is now
 Hindustan called.
All man-made Gods and Prophets of major
religions of world were her noble sons,
All known civilizations of world are now
linked with original Aryans.

In her glorious past, she was known as
      'The Golden Sparrow'.
Spirit of humanism, universal brotherhood
of mankind are integral parts of her
son's psyche like the bone and marrow.
Her sons had fathomed Great Sciences of Telepathy,
      Soulogy and Palmistry.
Modern scientists wonder at her 'Saint's, sage's & seer's
      inner depth, grasp and artistry.
She gave zero to the world
without which, Arithmetic would look so absurd.
Her language- 'Sanskrit' is the most scientific
      and complete one ever devised.
Greatest advancements of sound and phonetics in it, hide.
Her people don't dread death and consider
      it a part of continuity of life.
Smilingly they invite it for their self-respect
as, they recognize it as a basic human right.
Amidst the worst of calamities and hardships,
her people don't forget to do festival dance.
Remain always inwardly drawn to Him in trance.
Science of Yoga, meditation and herbal medicines
      are some of her beautiful gifts to world society.
Her culture preaches philosophy of rich
      soul in a healthy body in its entirety.
West is now learning 'YOGA' which India
      gifted to world innumerable centuries ago,
Match to Mahatma Gandhi's Weapon of
      'Ahinsa'[1] till date, West has nothing to show.
Today, India alone with her spiritual and
moral strength, can show the West path of
      world peace and Universal brotherhood.
Otherwise, amidst the galaxy of power hungry
and self centered nations, who could?

I'm sure, she would wage war for
    world peace with all her mite.
Her great role in achieving this laudable
    goal is well in sight.
All of us need to feel grateful and proud
    of the fact that we belong to this great soil.
For her lost glory, we need to rededicate
    ourselves and toil.
It's our moral duty today to preserve
    the fruits of our cultural heritage and
    extend it to others.
For that, we need to hold each other's hands
    and forge forward as brothers.
Let us live up to the expectations of our
    forefathers and kindle amongst us the
    spirit of national unity.
In it alone, lies real peace and progress
    of one 'n' all without any ambiguity.
Let us endeavour to make Her as great
    as she ever was!
Let us put our heart and soul in it
       Without a pause!
let us pledge ourselves to greet
each other by wishing 'Jai Hind' cheerfully with pride.
    And, tame all kinds of social and religious tide.
Martyrs of our Country gave their yesterday for our today.
'Jai Hind' 'Jai Hind' 'Jai Hind' Let
      us all in one voice say!

* * *

INDIAN SOLDIER

A living symbol of India's unity and integrity.
A replica of a perfect synthesis of her past and present in its
diversity.
Valour, sacrifice, dedication and devotion are his way of life
Knows how to toil through any strife.
His existence is for the Country's honour and glory.
There are no if & buts in his patriotic and valorous story.
Love of his Country and countrymen is his only passion.
Intense battlefield is his only mansion.
Derives inspiration and motivation from
Shivaji, Rana Pratap, Guru Gobind and Tipu Sultan.
Is ever ready to fulfill dreams of his Hindustan.
A devotee of Shakti, Durga and Shiva who, becomes all in one
when faces any enemy in battlefield.
Duty consciousness, self discipline, loyalty and patriotism are
then his body shield.
Knows how to humble and yet respect
any chivalrous enemy in the world.
His battle cry is like a lion's roar for a sheep herd.
Through the annals of his glorious military history,
has given ample proof of his forbearance, fortitude and sincerity.
He's ever ready to save his countrymen form all kinds of natural calamity.
He's a true 'Karmayogi'[2] and 'Gita'[3] in action.
inching forward in the enemy lines alone, gives him satisfaction.
He has exhibited professionalism, dedication of rare order on
glaciers, snow capped peaks, mountains, jungles, plains, deserts
and islands.
Proven worthy of both friend and foe's bouquets and garlands.
Has always reinforced his country men's faith and confidence.
Daring dauntless and courageous death in battle
is the epitome of his life's essence.

Today, he is the living symbol of disciplined and vibrant
Indian youth.
All set to preserve her unity, integrity and sovereignty
from evil designs of devilish sleuths.
Life and death for him, have no meaning.
Unfolding martial traditions of his army keep his spirits high
and gleaming.
For him, National Flag is the symbol of his very existence.
Security of every inch of motherland is
the only aim of his subsistence.
His hands symbolize devotion and mite.
He's determined to add glorious chapters to Free India's
History without a respite.
He well knows, that the whole nation respects
and backs him regardless of caste and creed.
Therefore, laying down life for other, is beyond the preview
of any selfish motive or greed.
Braves in peace war ribbons on the uniform with honour and pride.
All that is good in our culture and heritage, in him, hide.
Let us all care for him both in war and peace
and strengthen his hands and resolve.
It is then alone, any kinds of national crisis, will he, with ease, solve.
Let us give him in our society, a place of honour and dignity!
Since, he is a true Kshatriya[4]
imbued with power and magnanimity.

* * *

STRANGE LOYALTIES

Earth around me shakes when they plume,
I'm amidst whizzing bullets, flying splinters,
dust, smoke and war booms.
Enemy is trying to scare me with his fury and ferocity.
I'm getting determined to brave his steel on
my chest with strange curiosity.
You knew before accepting, me, I was already
married to profession of arms.
During peace times, I remained loyal to both but, now,
absolute loyalty to profession alone, the situation demands.
If I hesitate and don't rise to the occasion,
my comrades will call me coward.
With shattered ego in life, I won't be able to inch forward.
I think of you and all others who infused
strength in me to face this moment.
I must prove to my foe that he has touched a live wire
And infuriated a soldier; professionally potent.
Basic human weaknesses are many-folding war
and consequent death psychosis.
My inaction or impaired vision now, will cause untold losses.
May be, this is the last time you hear from me!
I am sure my nation and organization will look after thee.
I must act now with unflinching determination
lest, he under-estimates me and my comrades.
We'll soon, with one war cry, let lose our tirade.
It I don't return, you'll be a proud war-widow.
If I do, you'll be a proud wife of a victorious hero.

Tell ours when they grow up that their dad
laid down his life facing enemy in an active front.
So that, they in turn, face rough tides of life without a grunt.
Pray that I courageously challenge him, kill him or
kiss martyrdom valiantly.
We are all forging ahead to make our foe
experience our battle dexterity.
Hope, despite my savage and animal instincts, I prove humane!
I must believe that there are scruples even,
in our bloody game.
It's a well matched duel,
patriotism and loyalty are our fuel.
We'll fight unto our last as death comes only once to the brave.
What a befitting tribute, the whole nation pays;
Respects with fond memories at his grave!

* * *

CRYING NEED OF THE HOUR

It is discipline, which, weaves sounds of
various orchestra instruments into a symphony.
It is this alone, which, can restore in any mixed society
meaningful harmony.
It regulates day and night without amiss.
Differentiates between a lover's and rapist's kiss.
It is discipline which ensures life
in so many fascinating forms.
That's why, a corn seed produces only corns.
It is enshrined throughout the nature,
It is part of body rhythm of every creature.
It is discipline, which makes soldiers click heels together.
Even stinking hide, when disciplined, turns into useful leather.
Our sun with numerous satellites go on
revolving around their own and travel
billions of miles in fixed orbits in space.
Imagine, if there were indiscipline out there,
our entire solar system could
collapse in a great haste.
The presence of this element, determines
the cultural standard of any society.
Without it, no nation, no matter how big and rich,
can ever become mighty.
Need of the hour for all of us, is self discipline.
Otherwise, our land will stink like
an unattended garbage bin.
All of us have to inculcate it in our lives.
Remember, that's how, honey gets
stored up in bee-hives!

* * *

WAKE UP MY COUNTRYMEN!

Where have my countrymen gone
who, fought the mightiest of empires
and won freedom for their motherland?
Where are the patriots who braved bullets,
suffered baton blows and kept their lives
for all of us on the palm of their hand?
Where are those saint-soldiers who, through non-violence,
shook the British empire?
Where are those heroes who, pulled our Country
through a violent and turbulent quagmire?
Where are those wizards who, shaped our destinies
with honour and dignity?
Where are those nationalists who, ushered for all of us
an era of peace, progress and prosperity?
Where has that euphoria, zeal and national fervor
of all Indians gone which, freed us from shackles
and pangs of slavery?
Where are the chapters of our national freedom struggle
which, were written in golden letters
by our martyr's blood and bravery?
Do they today, only deserve to be given a
God-forsaken slot in our memory?
Nay! That would tantamount to treachery
with our collective culture and glorious history.
Our forefathers were unusually one,
both in thought and deed in waging
a relentless struggle for our freedom.
They'd unflinching faith in our
generation's collective wisdom.
Father of the nation laid foundations of Ram Rajya[5]
for us with truth and non-violence.

We, the ungrateful of all, have left no stone unturned
in putting shame to his benevolence.
If he were to get a chance to visit us, from heavens now,
with that painful murky quiver, he'll keep asking
everyone of us, the 'why' and 'how'?
Today, everyone thinks of himself and his near ones,
alas! no one about his nation.
Those in power and imbued with authority, are only,
filling their houses shamelessly without any hesitation.
Vested interest seekers have morbid the entire atmosphere
to such an extent that people draw swords
at flimsy grounds.
The suffering and privations of teaming millions
unabated knows no bounds.
We've divorced our culture, its rich heritage
and learnt no lessons from our history.
Surely at this rate, we'll turn this great land
into a great cemetery.
Our enemies across the immediate borders
are celebrating our foolishness.
They await a chance when, they'll turn tables
with a master stroke of cunningness.
I ask you my countrymen, one plain candid question;
What if you amass millions by hook or crook
when your motherland is most unsafe?
What if you make bombs and buy latest state of the art war
implements, when, your personal defenses cave?
What good is that freedom if parents,
when children are out of the house,
keep praying for their safe return?
Our innumerable sisters for want of money
and dowry, burn!
Farmers die for want of grain.
Educated and qualified drift away as part of brain- drain.
Terrorism, barbarism, cruelty and savagery haunts
at every one's door.

Gun wielding ultras hunt down poor
hapless innocent like, wild boar.
Today, we're dancing to the tunes of our enemies
both within and without.
At this rate, the day isn't far when our mothers
sisters, wives and daughters, in front of our eyes,
forcibly will lie on enemy's couch.
This way, we're bound to sell our bountiful motherland
most ignominiously, bit by bit.
Is it the way we should realize the value of our freedom,
since we haven't toiled for it?
All of us with concerted effort, could see through our country
out of the present mess.
Uphold the golden principle of secularism in thought
and deed and do our best.
The whole world is watching us,
if we fail, we disintegrate and get back
to days of abject slavery.
Our coming generations will mock at us
for our un-patriotism and treachery.
Little time is still there to mend our ways.
Otherwise, we' re all in for utterly
dark and dismal days.
I ask you which religion teaches us to live
the way anyone of us do?
We should be ashamed of ourselves as,
upon the sacred land of Buddha and Mahavira,
all kinds of violence we brew.
National flag of our great country exists
as here exist Hindus, Muslims, Sikhs
and Christians all alike.
We have to build a strong, formidable collective
national psyche.
Poverty, illiteracy, natural calamities are our
common enemies whom, we've to fight with all our mite.

Remember, in unity alone,
the future of our benign motherland is bright.
Think of chunks of our sacred mother land
which, still reel under enemy's suzerainty.
Disunity amongst us on parochial vested gains.
by a few, for all of us, will be our worst calamity.
Let us all take a vow to be proud of being Indian
and repay befittingly the toil and blood of our forefathers!
Wedge forward collectively with one firm resolve
without any bothers.
A betel leaf with four basic ingredients in various quantities
alone, becomes worth a chew.
Analogously, Hindus, Muslims, Sikhs and Christians
are for our national flagship, the basic and irreplaceable crew.
We can't afford to estrange anyone out.
On this account, let there be no doubt.
Pundit Jawaharlal on 15th August 47, announced
substantial fulfillment of an Indian's dream.
After 66 years, we; his beloved Indians are aiming at
each other's throat and make one 'n' all scream.
At the stroke of mid-night hour, after a prolonged struggle
on 15th August 47, while world slept,
India, awoke to freedom.
Look at us, what have we made out of that
hard earned kingdom!
Our children will weigh our deeds and misdeeds
and hold us squarely responsible for this great mess,
that they bequeath.
Undoubtedly, our actions will dictate how well
and how long they breathe.
My hope lie in our youth, which is
matured and pragmatic.
I appeal to them to do their best and prevent
our story from turning more tragic!

* * *

CODE OF CONDUCT

Those, who inflame communalism in a secular state,
play a dirty game.
No patriotic citizen would ever do that worth his name.
Those, who excite and arouse sentiments for vested interests,
are real traitors.
Their aim is only to retard country's progress and create craters.
Those, who kill innocents, perpetuate and precipitate fear
and commit dastardly crimes.
are the real devils of our times.
Those who usurp power through corrupt means
and spread corruption.
are undoubtedly worst offenders and deserve
only ruthless public prosecution.
Those public servants, who take bribes
for discharging their duty & Cause disenchantments
& dissatisfactions amongst public,
must be on the spot ignominiously cashiered from service.
Those, who evade taxes and file a wrong return,
Only, through long hard labour spells, must learn.
True practice of nationalism, patriotism and loyalty
of all Indians can only save this sinking ship
from a catastrophic disaster.
Wisdom lies in preserving our freedom and continuance in being
our own master
Those, who sing praises of enemy and live within,
should be gifted to the enemy for their worst sin.

Those, who live in our Country,
must be prepared to live & die for it.
Otherwise, this great nation will disintegrate and
fragment bit by bit.
Remember, preservation of internal security is the primary duty
of every citizen of our great nation,
In doing so, if one loses one's life, let there be absolutely no hesitation!

* * *

JUST THINK WHAT ARE WE UP TO?

I wonder why don't we have
some time to think about those,
Who sacrificed their lives in
defending our mother-land!
About those who dedicated their
lives for our freedom & left their
foot prints behind on our sand!
We are busy for power, money & selfish ends.
For such pursuits, we want to
follow short cuts, straight roads
without round about & bends.
Interest of our great nation doesn't occur to most of us today.
Only, 'Self' reins heart &
mind & some, don't hesitate in
doing away with those, who stand in their way.
Our enemies have already made
inroads exploiting our poverty
illiteracy, lack of patriotism, & inter-
religious sentiments.
At this crucial moment, I foresee a
Great civil war & enormous
blood-shed on the land of Buddha & Gandhi
as part of my presentiment.
We seem to have totally forgotten
a hard fact of our recent history,
whereby, the British slaved us in the same manner.
As different races, castes &
religious groups, we remained on our great continent
divided & steadfastly stood by different many a banner.

Are we going to repeat the same baneful atrocious story,
forgetting our great Indian Cultural heritage & glory?
If it happens, it would be the most tragic &
sordid story.
our future lies in the hands of our young ones,
Who, have to discharge their
responsibilities collectively &
individually as true mother India's sons.
Our Doctors, engineers, scientists
go & serve foreigners on the pretext of having
better life.
Our country's resources made them
what they are, but what a
tragedy, for our fellow Indians,
they aren't willing to put up strife.
Unemployment, poverty, illiteracy
& narrow vested interests have
led some disgruntled youth to take
up arms against the state.
Their mentors, both from within &
without, are injecting in them, for
their own interests,
the venom of cruelty & hate.
They must realize good or bad, this
country is theirs.
There is no use digging past & splitting hairs.
With one resolve, under one
national flag, we have to as patriotic
Indians, prove to the world,
especially our enemies, our bona fides.
Real progress & prosperity of all
of us, in it, alone hides.
I'm sure we have the ability & will to so prove.

God of all Hindus, Muslims, Sikhs & Christians,
please bless all Indians with unity,
nationalism & pride for the country
So that, all of us hand in hand, in right
direction from now on, move!
Think what are we up to?

* * *

A CHALLENGE TO ALL INDIANS

Joint families often split
basically, when the elders don't
see writing on the wall,
& don't respond responsibly to
the changing time's call.
So is true, with nations
when their leaders & government officials
forget the genuine interests &
aspirations of their countrymen.
Then, even staunch nationalists
  lose their patience.
Result is utter fiasco & disaster,
no matter how big or strong is
the country, it, then, breaks up
  rather faster.
Religions, regionalism, language,
ethnic background, poverty,
backwardness then, propel society
towards bloodiest of carnage.
Erstwhile nationals, then, get at
throats of each other in an
unprecedented show of anger & rage.
In a democratic country, where
secessionism, terrorism & cruel
carnage of innocents is an
  everyday affair.
Government officials & political leaders
must be made accountable
for making most undesirable
gross misuse of their chair.

These very people make rules &
then bend them for their
    personal gains
Add more confusion, distrust
affliction & drive innocent &
helpless citizens into insanes.
We need to have a rationale &
dispassionate look at
ourselves now, before it's too late.
If prevailing winds continue
unabated & unchecked, our
great country would fragment
further, rather fast, at this rate.
In modern times, democracy.
secularism & nationalism is the only
viable way of life for us all.
Therefore, let us all accept our
challenges ahead & pay heed to our
    Mother India's call!

* * *

BUBBLES OF TIME

I find times are just the same;
The British may have left,
many of our blood now, are eating
up the vitals of our country under
many a different name.
British as a system, believed
in 'Divide & Rule'.
For our corrupt high chair holders,
raking up religious passions, phony
and baseless promises and playing the card
of caste and creed for sticking to their chairs
are effective tools.
All of us, have to recognize soon
enough, our great nation's need,
& forget about all these narrow
and parochial visions!
Forge forward in steps, as true
patriotic Indians, forgetting self-
created divisions.
Two things have enormous significance today;
Nationalism and small family for
our bright future have a lot of say.
Nationalism would make one 'n' all
ready to do or die for our motherland.
Adherence to small family norm by
all, would ensure each one with an earning hand.
It's high time, all of us
collectively put an end to our
self-created pities, woes and cries.
Otherwise, our children would surely
pay for our misdeeds, an enormous price!

* * *

AFTER 66 YEARS OF INDEPENDENCE

Our country stands today at a crucial crossing
where, two distinct
roads exist; one of peace and progress
and the other of self annihilation and regress.
On one, all of us together
holding each other's hand can
tread singing our national song.
Whereas, on the other, militant bands
of caste, religious and separatist psyche
would kill each other most savagely before long,
Choice lies not with any one
individual, but with the masses,
Like, cattle chooses to have
a particular type out of different kinds of grasses.
At this juncture, our collective
decision is most vital,
like, most significant is,
assigning a theme, its apt title.
Our future, as a nation,
depends on what we all decide.
Like, married life to a great
extent, depends on the choice of the bride.
Once, we have got on to
any one road, there is no way
one can stage a come-back.
At the end of one road, we would
find our tricolour and on the
other, once again a Union Jack.

Before deciding, think of our
glorious past, great heritage, culture
and future of our young generation.
May Gods of all religions of
the world bless you my
Countrymen with Their benign
wisdom to avoid a path of
self destruction and degeneration!

* * *

FESTIVAL OF COLOURS

It denotes advent of the king of seasons; the spring
along with multiple colors,
new hopes, aspirations and joyful
optimism in everyone's life, It brings
all Indians regardless of
caste and creed embrace one 'n'
other & sprinkle dry and wet
colors with fond affections.
Nowhere else, in the world, one
could witness this joyful
frenzied, free and brotherly interaction.
On this festival, people after
offering colors to their Gods,
get together on streets and roads.
Children get busy in injecting
& spraying colorful waters in all kinds
     of modes.
In different colors and masks.
everyone looks more than funny.
Rejoicing and celebrations get a
fillip if the day turns out
     to be bright and sunny!
People sing songs while
beating all sorts of Bongos and Drums.
Celebrations are marked with
traditional gaiety, fervour and
joyous moods even in slums.
People forget their differences
and bury their past amidst
     a riot of colors.

Everyone gets in a gleeful mood
listens, narrates jokes, anecdotes
and howlers while having many a traditional food.
Some await moments when
they could feel the touch of
their heart throbs profusely
    under its pretext.
would she joyfully accept & reciprocate is
obviously their litmus-test.
Even terrorists join in the
celebrations with those, on their hit list
Even sworn enemies find time to play cards
with big bets with friendly gestures like sun rays & mist
On this day of fun and frolics,
everyone seems happy and full of life
and seem to forget their
days of agony, anguish and strife.
Females amongst themselves
have a lot of fun.
When cold and colorful waters
streak across and inside their
clothes, some show as if
    embarrassed and stunned.
Somewhere, men receive joyfully
rope lashings and bashings from
    their village females.
Colors are joyfully sprayed
even on passengers moving on
buses, cars, two wheelers and rails.
All Indians regardless of their
place celebrate this festival
with warmth, affections and
enjoy days together this
    great national festivity.

Such beautiful days undoubtedly
add to our great nation's esprit de corps,
sensitivity, longevity and unity
    in diversity.

* * *

INDIA IS OF ALL INDIANS

All 1.2 Billion humans of our
　　great nation are her real wealth.
Upon their inter-se-relation,
　　depends this country's health.
Blood that flows in the arteries
of Hindus, Muslims, Sikhs & Christians
　　is just the same.
There's a great commonality of
　　meanings behind our various many a name.
On the blood in all human
bodies, on our soil,
　　only, this country has the right.
Like, upon brightness, the
Exclusive right is that of source of light.
No one regardless of caste &
creed is justified to waste this blood.
Only, for the protection of this nation,
all of us, have the privilege
to offer it in the form of a great flood.
Our temples, mosques, Gurudwaras &
Churches are nothing but
　　masonry work in cement & bricks.
If we just term these as common religious places,
I think, it should do the trick!
All our sacred books preach us
to be a good neighbour & a good brother
If our religious prophets were alive,
I'm sure they would embrace each other!
When will we understand
　　the national needs?
& when will we understand and
perform for our country, selfless deeds?

* * *

BRAHMAPUTRA

Name suggests that, I' am the only male river.
Anyone who sees me, in or after Monsoons, gets a quiver.
I originate from the top seat of world
    where, even snows and ice shiver.
I'm the longest and of course, the strongest
whose, rapids, current and whirl pools
    churn up, anyone's liver.
I trickle out from the same area, of
    great pious lakes, from where, emerge river
Sindh & Satluj & my revered sister Ganges.[6]
Upon the area between our source and confluence, great
ancient Hindu civilization hinges
Invariably, I travel distant lands of my
valley, beyond my known banks, and give you
    a vivid glimpse of my fury and ferocity.
I admire those who set out to tame
my rapids, for their guts and audacity.
I nurture in my lap a variety of charming tribes,
whose lives beam out happy, healthy and contented vibes.
Heralding spring with skies so clear,
Assamese in my valley celebrate their new year.
Their mornings richly bathed, in fresh dew.
April is festive with 'Rangoli Bihu'[7]
Nestling in the lap of snow covered peaks,
with me, running still and deep.
They, all sing and dance with zest.
My lap, is indeed, in its splendid best.
As Bihu festival reaches climax,
    whole of my valley, gets in to a unique and remarkable mood.
All Assamese dance, sing, laugh, greet each
    other and taste many a traditional food.

On tunes of 'Bihu' vigorously they dance,
as if, their bodies and souls commune with Him
   in trance.
Somewhere, with 'Joy-de-vivre and gay abundant,
   Bodos sing Bagurumba'[8]
Fair maidens with their colourful scarfs,
   dance the local Rhumba
Sure-footed, vibrant and yet, shy
   they flit gracefully like butterflies.
Somewhere, in the months of March and April
with Yam and Paddy in Plains and on hill,
seeds of hope and happiness sprout.
With rhythmic beats of Ali-ai-ligung[9]
Mishings sing and dance in joyful moods-no doubt.
Somewhere, on scintillating and rejuvenated
   bamboo movements and sound,
Tiwas celebrate Takhrapalla Misuwa[10] by singing
and dancing, hand in hand, while going round and round.
Culminating into vigorous yet, rhythmic and
reverberating beats of drum and pipe,
mesmerizing on-lookers, right from its inception,
till it's absolutely ripe.
Their feet and body get into a majestic sway,
tasting feast of ecstasy and joy throughout night and day.
For your prosperity, I could be a factor
   substantially vital and influential.
It you could, just recognize and tap, only my hydel potential.
Through me, like in older times, you
could most economically transport, all time mercantile.
your ingenuity could help me reach,
distant dry lands which are otherwise fertile.
If you genuinely take interest in me,
I could usher in an era of great prosperity for all.

Otherwise, don't blame me, your progress, my anger would
    continue to stall.
Make maximum use of my waters and valley lands.
You would get Gold even out of my dry sands!
Remember, story of your great ancestors began on my banks.
Live and sing together regardless of file and ranks.
Whole of India is proud of you all.
Serve this great nation of ours like, I've been
since perennial year, is the times prime call.

* * *

COUNTRY IS NOT A THING TO PLAY WITH

What's happened to you oh, my countrymen?
You've completely forgotten that you are Indians
first and anyone else later.
Is it because our young generation without any suffering,
    got freedom right on the platter?
I've heard of mothers selling their babies in
    utter distress but,
never grown-ups selling their mother.
Most of you, at the moment, seem to be doing just
    that without a bother.
Some of you, live here and sing our enemy's praise.
Shouldn't you be bundled up and thrown across the border
Or in a public square be put to blaze?
Some of you, play with health and lives of fellow citizens.
Shame on you; shouldn't you be tied up in front
of public and roughed up by worst of goons and hooligans?
Some of you, in Government chairs, ask most
shamelessly, for doing duty, your share.
Shouldn't the public be given one free day with
you, for whatever treatment they can spare?
Some of you, think of only carving states out
of existing states and thus jam the wheels of any meaningful
progress.
Remember, by doing that you are only helping our
enemies and opening inroads of his ingress.
Some of you are foolish enough to think of our
common enemy to be as best friend and thus
visit him, get trained and return with arms to
commit most heinous crimes against your own kith and kin.
Shouldn't you all, be stored up in the city's largest
    refuge or garbage bin?

Some of you, win popular mandate and thereafter, fill
up own mansions forgetting all promises and resolution.
Shouldn't you be treated like Dukes, Barons and
Nobility were during the French Revolution?
If you don't mend your ways, whole Country will
be up in flames and become a place worst than Beirut
for miles together, not a single dog and an owl at
    night to hoot.
By forgetting our common heritage and culture, we'll
do the worst crime against our ancestors.
Look up at clear night sky and realize how all
heavenly bodies are staring at you as mute protestors.
Today, your actions please only our common foe:
They are celebrating and rejoicing our collective
foolishness as they achieve their goal without
    using a bow.
Forget regionalism, parochialism and filling up
Own houses by hook or crook and think only of
our great one nation.
Otherwise, your days are numbered; either you
would be dead on land or find yourself at the
bottom of deep Indian Ocean.
Time is running out.
There is no doubt.
Act now. Lest, it's too, late.
Remember, otherwise for your story, there'll neither
be a listener nor anyone to narrate.
Country isn't a thing to play with.

* * *

INDIAN WOMANHOOD

Dauntlessly courageous,
deeply religious.
An exquisite beauty,
always up and about for her duty.
Dedicated, sincere and loyal to her husband,
for her honor, ever-ready to take war like stand.
A strong pillar of any home.
most beautiful part of any monument
    like its dome.
Love, care and sacrifice amazingly in abundance,
benign compassion immensely intense.
Prefers death than disgrace,
shy of her own praise.
Replica of juvenile delinquent grandeur.
Her sagacity and devotion in the annals of our
    history is a subject of great lure.
Mai Bhago, Rani Jhansi and Padmini are some
of them, around whom, the glorious and
valiant Indian traditions are built.
In adversity, knows to hold her husband's
    hands rather than jilt.
She can brave poverty and privations.
In any home, a spring source of
    celebrations and jubilations
In abject poverty, she shares happily
her husband's sufferings and toils.
Is contented with the left-overs of the
family and at the end of a long day, on
    floor, gladly coils.

A source of great binding, power and motivation.
Silent builder of a great nation.
She certainly deserves respect and care and NOT
    maltreatment.
In it, lies great deal our cure and
    national honor, progress & aggrandizement.

* * *

SENTINEL OF INDIA; HIMALAYAS

Scintillating music of many a water fall,
trees and twines more than tall.
Wooden bridges over brooks,
rocks and stones with chiselled looks.
Purity of ice and water, that of blue sky,
birds of all sorts more than high.
Absolutely green valleys and mountains,
inter-woven with invisible chains.
Dancing and cajoling Trout,
Wild elephant, tiger, rhinoceros, spotted deer, bear and
      boar with well developed snout.
Winged colors in wild flights,
blue perennial ice on great heights.
Flowers of incredible variety,
boulders, stones, cliffs; massive and mighty.
hearts pure and simple,
tribals with smiles and dimple.
Breeze; unusually fragrant and musky,
ecological jazz; bone thrilling and husky.
Air naturally clean and
wild flower everywhere for sure.
Nature in its pristine pure
Fascinating glaciers and many a towering virgin peak.
True peace, many hermits and sages, through penance and
renunciation in your lap, seek.
Valleys, both misty and bright.
Straight cliffs and rocks invite spontaneous shriek and fright.
Great lakes and blue water sources,
innumerable water channels making their courses.
Man and pristine nature in great harmony
amidst abundance of natural food and honey.
Human warmth, natural tranquility in no dearth..

Indeed, heavenly abode on our earth.
In you, pristine, untouched natural beauty hide.
For all Indians, you're a great source of joy
    and national pride.
Hey! Now let me say,
"Use your ingenuity and tap my hydroelectric potentials.
With power in abundance, you could establish for
yourself in the world new credentials.
You, yet don't know the mineral ores, precious treasures
that lie within my fold.
You could unravel the flood gates
to unlimited mighty stores of Uranium, Iridium
Luthenium, Aluminum, Diamonds & Gold.
Don't let me be grabbed & taken over
bit by bit by anyone thinking that, after
all, these are inhospitable, uninhabited
barren pieces of desolate lands
At this rate, your enemies would soon chop your feet & hands.
Remember, if I'm in your possession, you could survive.
Otherwise, it would be impossible to get into Indian ocean & hide.
I'm still known by the name given to me by your ancestors &
therefore, only you & only you, in the world, have over me,
birth right.
Therefore, as a nation for the national glory &
pride be prepared at
all times to wage a massive fight!
Remember, peace in this world, can only
be negotiated from the position of national strength.
Therefore, be one regardless of caste & creed
both in thought & deed throughout your breadth & length.
Don't sell or barter me for few chips stacked in foreign lands.
Remember, your sworn enemies won't spare
you even when you are requesting to spare
your lives with folded hands!

* * *

QUIT INDIA MOVEMENT

In Year 1942, India witnessed Indian
    masse's great resolve;
A problem, which the British couldn't solve.
Under Mahatma Gandhi; Father of the
nation in making, whole country was just one
That's why,
a great colonial power in whose empire,
sun never set, was on the run.
Regardless of religion, caste & creed
all Indian's equivocally were behind the
    movement's aim
Our Rulers buckled under its pressures & became
    timid and tame.
Display of unprecedented non-violent mass movement of all
Indians forced Colonialists to take stock of things
    well in time.
Bowing to the collective will of masses was then,
Only graceful alternative by way of which, the
British could get back with all jewels and dime!
Nearly, after seven decades, there's a greater
need in our free country to display another
    similar movement;
This time, against poverty, illiteracy, corruption,
regionalism & separatism for the sake of
meaningful in real time, India's all-round improvement.
We have to, once again, display our
collective wisdom and will towards this end.
Rise above our selfish motives and therefore,
    ways and means we must mend.

For this goal, any amount of sacrifice, we should be
    prepared to give.
That's how, we could all in free India,
    Continue to live.
It's as noble a cause as it was then.
Otherwise, all of us would once again,
hear in our country, the sounds of Big Ben!

* * *

HISTORY LESSONS

Why do we learn history?
I suppose, to solve our past riddles, puzzles
    and mystery
Our abject slavery for centuries
was undoubtedly due to disunity,
which, was exploited by foreigners
    with a great impunity.
It was our collective resolve alone
which, has made us breathe free air.
Alas! Over the years of independence,
most of us, for selfish ends, are running after
    only powers and an influential chair.
Our wide cross section of society
is once again disunited and looking
    in different directions.
For vested interests, there're armed
    struggles, insurgencies and insurrections.
We Should burn our history books
    since, we haven't learnt from our past.
Surely, at this rate, we're going to get back
into days of slavery rather fast.
A golden lesson that emerges from
our history is that, unity is strength'
Without which, our country will
    go to dogs and stench.
Beautiful fertile lands remain untilled
Then, lazy people crib & ask
how many due to poverty, on their lands every year
    get perished and killed.
Somewhere, people believe in only Kharif[11]
    & of course, central Government's relief.

How would that region prosper
    with this kind of popular belief?
If our country has to continue to be independent
we all, regardless of caste and creed, have to
    remain united and one.
Shun laziness, disloyalty towards nation
      and not pick up, for own
      selfish motive, a gun.

* * *

THINK FOR A WHILE

We must know that :-

Administration devoid of enforcement, is impotence.

Application of force in the absence of administration is
    another expression of tyrannical intolerance.

Bigoted religiosity for vested interest, can cause death knell
    to a nation.

Like, lack of spirit of give & take, can mar the warmth in any
    human relation.

Instead of vulgar abuse of muscle, money, media, positional &
    political power.

respect for sovereignty of rule of law, logic & merit
    is the need of hour.

Feudalism with 'Maharaja Culture' Could eat the very
    basis of democratic society.

Like, egoism would kill in anyone, sobriety.

'Touch me not', ethos of an individual, group or party
    sans any logic.

& can lead to ends; most tragic.

Exploitation of decent & simple folks of Indian
    citizenry is the greatest sin & and act of disloyalty.

Like vulgarity in public, can spoil the very image of any royalty.

If, we don't be careful, we may overturn over bends!

Our country possesses mammoth resilience & potentials,

provided, we stand united & prove our credentials!

* * *

GOLDEN GATE

In our country today, dilution of work
    culture is the biggest bane.
We have tucked in Lord Krishna's Golden words;
Do your duty & leave the rest to me' in some obscure memory lane.
As & when, Government officials & politicians called public
servant's actions san any service.
all efforts are then, going to be lop sided & amiss.
If, occupants of high chairs think that money &
merry making alone is their sole-propriety,
result is bound to be a disaster & general break-down of
any system, no matter how scientific, organized for the society.
Due to this, majority suffers as if, under heavy loads of tons.
Some out of them, resign to their lot & suffer in
silence but some, resort to guns.
In such environment, peace of both the administrator
& the administered is sure to be lost.
Inevitably for which, the whole nation then, pays a very
    heavy cost.
Any meaningful foundation of work culture is
laid both at home & school.
Mental make-up is directly proportional to what child
observes around him in his impressionable age as a thumb rule.
Therefore, to that end. Parents & teachers of our & next
generation have a great responsibility to discharge.
Without which, real peace & prosperity of our
great country would remain at large.

Let us build a golden gate like in U.S. West Bay
where, blue sea waves dance perpetually with bright sun ray.
Also, where musky, fragrant & friendly breeze blow,
year long to & fro.
we, too, can do it if, we have collective will.
Otherwise, how long we hope to be alive lying on
     a live grill!

* * *

SPIRITUALISM

MY GRACIOUS LORD

How can you forget Thy glory?
As ordained, I began my story.
You're potter and self in your dexterous hands, mere clay.
You could mould me in any way.
I'm your worshipper, devotee and an ardent fan.
Just keep me at your door steps, if you can.
Your blessings are countless indeed.
How about keeping me far away from hatred and greed?
Mother, Father, Brother, Sister, Wife, Son, Daughter, Friend
and foe are all your manifestation.
Shouldn't service to poor, leper, deaf and dumb & a destitute
be a source of my recreation?
My only immutable Saviour, when seas are high and rough.
How I Wish I're nearer to you than myself.
I, in order to remember you every breath
certainly need your gracious help
Decidedly my spiritual needs are far greater than physical,
without loving your creation, my chances of seeing you are
remote and dismal.
Your graces and ways to me, are a great mystery.
Please bestow upon me insight to understand my own chemistry.
I want to talk to you without my lips playing any part.
Want to establish a direct uninterrupted
communication through my heart.
Living with you and loving your creation is heavenly bliss.
I'll keep waiting for blessed moments when your feet, I,
could kiss.
I'm a passing pilgrim and you, my destination.
You're my forgotten heritage and therefore, I seek a direct
relation.
You, oh my lord, are my refuge and solace,
the only caretaker for this hopeless case.

Those, who doubt your existence, hurl greatest insult,
Please keep me away from them and their cult.
Having separated me, you've created many a pseudo attraction.
Tell me, for how long, will be our separation?
Like fire dispels darkness, gives warmth and destroys cold.
Chastise me with your divine wisdom, and make me, in your
service, more bold.
In order to see, hear and experience Thee, Surely, I need
benign guidance.
Otherwise, how would I retrieve my lost inheritance?

* * *

A COMMON GOAL

I watched pilgrims reaching a shrine
from many a direction.
I saw many a river near sea in a great
interaction.
In both cases, goal is one but, more than one ways
like, sun is one but, innumerable rays.
Similarly, Union with god and with all things
In Him, is the goal of all mankind.
In order to realize Him, we leave many foot prints
on different paths and ways behind.
Life has no meaning other than conscientious
realization of our oneness with god
Our relationship is analogous to a piece of cloth
with a color, symbol and a rod.
At the end of the road, what good is it
if you are spiritually a bankrupt?
When you know well that all throughout, ways
to amass wealth had been more than corrupt!
Remember, your birth-right is immortality.
For that, live with Him and shun all kinds of duality.
Love, no doubt is panacea of all ills.
Egoism, hatred, greed and desire, most savagely, it kills.
Therefore, why not just love everyone around
& realize Him before claiming six feet of ground?

* * *

DELIGHTS OF YOUR NEARNESS

Delights of your nearness are innumerable,
some describable and some inexplicable.
It's the pleasure of having rain bath in summer,
sight of good spikes to a short distance runner,
It's the happiness of holding new born for the
first time by any mother.
For a lonely girl, the sight of her lost brother,
It's the delight of a blind when he
Gets the touch of his walking stick
sight of a tough match winning kick,
It's the privilege of doing job to one's satisfaction,
sight of a gymnast giving performance
of ten-point perfection.
It's the fillip to an artist's spirits when
his work gets recognition.
For a ship-wrecked, sight of an inhabitation.
It's the sensation sparked with magic touch of
Angel's hand.
Sight of heart throb in far distant land.
I must admit, your nearness to me is,
an experience out of this world.
I won't let you go away from me if, I could!

* * *

FAITH MOVES MOUNTAINS

Don't get demoralized if, he doesn't listen.
Remembering Him & thanking Him for all
His blessings, should only be your mission.
Have faith, He would respond one day,
hopefully, soon enough. till then, have patience
maintain balance & don't get rough.
Take His name with every breath as long as he makes you breathe.
In the next life, invaluable wealth of His name
you must bequeath.
Most of us waste this life in empty conversation.
We must request Him for yet another chance.
with a total transformation.
Without faith in Him, you could, only hoodwink self
& how long could you go on?
With faith in Him, you could experience solace, delight
& blissful happiness with all dark clouds around you gone.
He is One with different names.
What a pity! followers of his various names are playing
all over the world such dirty games!
Have mercy on us & through some divine massage,
tell 'one-a-all' that Allah, Ishwar, Christ & Nanak
are all one God's manifestations
So that all of us, embrace each other with love & affection
without any hesitations.
This life is incredibly valuable because, In this form alone,
you could do selfless service for those, who suffer.
Without realizing, it, believe you me,
it's a life of an absolute duffer.

* * *

MY PRAYER

God, oh God! I desire of you universal peace
and good of all on our beautiful earth!
Sensitize us with human compassion and
redesign turbulence in our heart,
so that, all of us peacefully, with love for one
and other, could play our part.
Energize us
so that, we actively engage in 'service before self' without a fuss,
Bless rich a bit of poverty
and poor a bit of richness
so that, we could experience each other's sickness.
Give us feelings to understand the suffering
humanity's woes.
so that, we could put an end to our hate and
hypocrisy ridden life cruise.
Kindle our hearts with love of humanity,
So that, we wipe out caste, color and creed lunacy.
Enlighten us with your wisdom,
So that, we could fathom and preserve our
Nature's blissful kingdom.
Chastise our religious preachers,
So that, they honestly profess universal love
for all living creatures.
Dispel our self created fears and infuse confidence,
So that, we may uphold human dignity
exhibit patience.
Convert us into your true image,
so that, all of us could cooperate and lend
helping hand to wipe out affliction.
Revitalize our ears to listen inner promptings of conscience,
so that, we don't remain slothed
in religious bigotry, dogmas and pretence.

Bestow upon us the sense of sharing our joys and other's
sufferings regardless of artificial man-made barriers,
so that, we could blow out suffocation here and
venture in space as universal peace carriers.
Guide us, lest, we get trapped in materialistic delusion,
so that we may see everything through
your divine vision.
Bless peace for everyone.
Have mercy on us and please accept each one of us
as, your own daughter or son.

* * *

A DROP IN A STREAM AND ME

I was where the blues of perennial ice & sky meet.
He ordained & a drop melted with His divine heat.
I was in the purest form of my existence &
His spark in me made me move.
With His predestined path, of course unknown to me,
I trickled out of a groove.
Pure & fresh, I was like part of His subsistence.
& bade good bye to my heavenly mother bed.
My past of heavenly solace & bliss was now dead.
I fell into waiting hands of many a drop
who had collected in a small pool.
As I came amidst their existence.
I noised peculiarly & lost my cool.
Other drops had trickled from sources both
known & unknown.
Our temperatures, frequencies & inherent energies
were identical as we're all His own.
I'd the potential of boundless energy & was extremely active.
I stirred out with others for unknown destination.
Of course, exactly as He pre-set it within
His frame of creation.
I danced & bounced from one bank to another
made all kinds of sounds on hitting boulders
& jumping on & with other.
We made fun of boulders, trying to stop us by circumventing.
At time, chiselled through rocks & roots & went on gallivanting.
We're collectively & gradually growing bigger in size,
with ever increasing momentum on the set cruise,
we're fast losing spiritual height which,
of course, we didn't realize.

Constant frictions within & without rose my temperatures
When, I looked back on those heavenly dizzy heights.
of my origin, I Could only cry at my present stature.
It's now no longer clean & pure.
My downfall will go on unabated, I was sure.
I, now, started pondering amidst all kinds of dirt around
& over my rim.
How to get back & be with Him!
The possibility obviously looked rather remote & dim.
I'll have to do penance For this dirty game!
& let my form suffer intense heat.
Hopefully to be drifted back with right kind of wind, indeed.
If ever, I get back from where I came,
shall pray to Him not to send me again.
For this dirty game!

* * *

AN HUMBLE REQUEST

Where should I post you my letter and on which address?
No one other than you.
can give this suffering humanity, a redress.
I hear, you are omnipresent and omnipotent.
Why don't you then, sort out cruel butchers of the
innocents and are hesitant?
I bet killing innumerable innocents all over the world,
can't give you any pleasure.
Somehow, you've to put an end to it.
perhaps, by some divine measure.
You must prove worthy of your name
and come up-to hapless suffering humanity's expectations.
Otherwise, they will suffer not only painful death,
but, all sorts of indignation.
They are your and in you alone, trust.
Somehow, restore order and civility, soon enough,
which you must.
If savage fanaticism is the most important part of religion,
then, let there be none.
If killing hapless innocent children,Woman and Men
is a religious act and right of some, then, give everyone a gun
Everyone seems to be losing sanity and balance.
Do you know life has become unusually and enormously tense?
I request thee to act fast.
otherwise, faith in you won't last.
You, alone, could bring drastic reformation of everyone's heart
and mind.
Please prove to us before it's too late that you're
graciously benevolent and most kind.

* * *

YOU'RE OMNIPRESENT

I here you in the sounds of mountain brooks.
I feel your affections when, for, me, my mother cooks.
I see you in the smiles of an infant.
I experience your beauty, when I behold my
Heart throb in bewilderment.
I see your anger, when typhoons, ravage lands
And volcanoes blow.
I see your tranquility, when tides, are low.
I realize your big heart when you take birth amongst us,
establish Dharma and lead us to righteousness.
I realize your greatness,
when a seed, sprouts out of soil.
I See your agility when a Cobra, hoods out of his coil.
I get aware of you when, I see an old,
I experience depression when towards me,
You suddenly turn cold.
I detest your directions, when, man turns a beast.
I admire you, when your followers taste a divine feast.
To me, branches of a massive tree; laden with fruit and
hugging ground, denote your humility,
a sun-rise on seas, your serenity.
I see you, hear you and feel you everywhere.
Don't I deserve Your personal care?

* * *

FALSE SENSE OF CLEANLINESS

You cleanse your body many times a day without fail,
rub oils, use soaps, perfumes even shape and polish your nail.
Adore yourself in front of mirrors hours together.
Wear matching clothes to suit occasion,
time of day and weather.
All this, may glorify your outer cast.
whereas, cleaning the inside, which is, more vital,
conveniently you forgot.
Cooking utensils need to be cleaned from inside first.
Similarly, remove dirt from heart & mind by
good and civilized conduct you must.
There is a definite need to clean
both these vital parts.
As, these dictate your actions which,
can win other's hearts.
Remember, effects of perfumes and toiletry
on outer skin, are only transitory.
whereas, on heart and mind; permanent & salutary.
Those, who remain clean from inside,
don't really require such outer applications.
Their skin unusually glows and radiates without
any make-up and elaborate preparations.
There's a need to reconsider the very concept of cleanliness.
As cleanliness from inside, could wipe out altogether
your weariness & tardiness.
Spending so much of time and money
for only outside appearance, to me,
is a sheer waste.

Remember, any language appeals only
when it's idiomatic and chaste.
Also, any food appeals only, when it, smells
Good and is rich in taste.
Your outer appearance could possibly befool a few.
How about cleaning the inside
in order to become pearl out of dew?

* * *

BALANCE SHEET

One day, you're bound to get His invitation.
Thereafter, there is no room for your excuse or protestation.
That will be His first and last one.
You'll of course, receive it all of a sudden.
You shall have to go there.
Leaving behind, all that is here.
You can't carry any gifts to please and placate.
In His presence, an accurate account of your deeds
will be read out as on that date.
Your enclosure in that gathering, will be
according to your classification.
His decision in this regard, is final
over which, there is no court with jurisdiction.
You alone, could ensure that, you carry balance
in your account sheet not in red.
For that, only selfless service of suffering humanity
is the best bet.
Therefore, how about changing without wasting
any more time, your very outlook & mentality!
He'll then, receive you himself and extend
graciously all his divine hospitality!

* * *

HOW ABOUT THIS WAY!

If you remember always and
everywhere, God and death
seek divine pleasures through
the span of each breath,
genuinely care for your spiritual
    health,
Then, you'll never feel the
    dearth of real wealth.
We forget that, He resides
nowhere else than inside,
like within sea itself, reside
    all kinds of tide.
No one can ever imagine looking
at top surface of sea water, how
beautiful could be beneath.
Similarly, no one can ever
even dream of unexplored
marvelous world, that lies
within the body shield.
Rhythm and melody of inner sounds,
of brain and heart, are beyond anyone's wildest guess.
It's only, when they rattle around
and produce jarring notes, that one
finds oneself in a veritable mess.
By diving deep inside darkness alone,
one can realize the most
fascinating spectrum and panorama
    of unimaginable shades and lights.
Like, how charmingly magnificent
is our planet, one can only realize
it from great heights.

There is enormous beauty both in
and around
as, His benign beauty knows no bound.
In order to seek divine beauty
and truth, we need to train our
    eyes and vision,
so that, we could perceive it
    out of all worldly delusion.

* * *

GREATEST OF ALL

Sun, Moon and Stars sparkle with thy Light,
countless stars and planets in billion of universes
revolve around and move with Thy might.
Life exists in millions of forms
    with Thy artistic dexterity,
breathing is there with Thy mercy and benign charity.
Finger prints speak of Thy architectural talents.
Wonders of our and other worlds are Thy patents.
Flowers and their fragrance denote Thy magnanimity,
a limitless empire is under Thy direct suzerainty.
Blood flows in body with Thy will and desire.
It remains warm with Thy fire.
Principle of ecological balance of life is
    Thy magical creation,
sensory organs of body get
    energized with Thy sensation.
If you've created such big universes,
I wonder what would be Your size!
Yet, I know you reside in each one's
heart and personally guide.
Thou are omnipotent, omnipresent
    & mightiest of all.
Those, who believe in this
universal truth only, can hear and respond
to Thy promptings and call!!

* * *

SPIRITUAL PROGRESS

This life is too short to
understand Him & His creation.
Spiritual progress from very early
age alone, can lead one to
Some sort of emancipation.
Most of us think of Him
only, when we're near our end.
Therefore, we're neither
this side nor the other side
of that road bend.
When no one has time for one,
then alone, one
tries to speak to Him,
not realizing that for such
a late start, prospects of
winning spiritual race are rather dim.
Progressively if one, devotes
some time with Him from
an early age, one can
make meaningful spiritual headway.
Otherwise, it's futile
dreaming about seeing
at the fag-end, that divine ray.
Degree of spiritual success
depends. No doubt, on the
earnest efforts made,
like, a hired laborer at the end
of the day, surely gets paid.
It's a fallacy to think that,
materialistic & Spiritual
progress can't go on side by side.

Remember, both pleasure & body exercise are
inherent in a horse-ride.
For understanding Him,
each breath is important.
For a direct dialogue, one
has to suffer body pain & torment.
Life in human form
without understanding Him,
is a sheer waste.
One has to be prepared
to suffer all kinds of
privations on order to
get that Divine taste.

* * *

TO ME, YOU'RE EVERYTHING

If you're with me, why should I fear?
I'm grateful beyond words because, you're so near/
You've given me everything as if, I was your own.
Your benign healing touches tickle the inside of my bone.
My wealth can't diminish even if, I spend by millions a day.
Like, the great sun can never be without a light ray.
Because of you, there are no unmanageable challenges &
    privations in life.
That's why in seemingly difficult times, I've a smile.
Like, warm clothes don't make a dead body warm,
under Your protection, no one can cause me any harm.
Without You, no one would like me and care.
Under Your feet, there are pleasures and happiness, indeed rare.
It would be my privilege to be your pet.
Your affectionate pats then, I can safely hope to get.
Would get a chance to see you and be called by my first name.
That's exactly my cycle of birth and rebirth's aim.
Please keep me kindled with your benign vision.
For my soul, a meeting with you is going to be a most
    privileged occasion.

* * *

GOD- HOOD

Godhood is;-
    Mother's concern for her son,
    over snow and ice, heat and brightness of sun,
    aim behind a gun,
    spirit of dedication & devotion in a missionary nun,
    charms of pristine nature,
    aesthetic sense behind caricature,
    faith of a believer,
    architectural talents of a Beaver,
    strength in arms,
    lines on palms,
    smiles and cries of a new born,
    happiness of a farmer when,
    he beholds his field, full of corn,
    wild flower's beauty and fragrance,
    bewitching charms of a jungle; dense,
    Instant milk in mother's breast,
    spirits of excelsior in a child in a test,
    blush of a young maid,
    courageous spirits behind a daring commando raid.
    spirit behind innovation,
    feeling of elation,
    flow in life,
    sense of loyalty in an Indian wife,
    sharpness of Knife,
    protection and care in mother's womb,
    spirit behind temple and mosque's tomb.

* * *

LOVE OF GOD!

Silver of moon-light,
musky and marshy odor over brimming
salt-tide.
Flight of lark full of verve at great height,
mocking bird's piercing song through the
stillness of moon-lit night,
avid brightness of milky way,
mammoth energy behind each Sun's ray,
lamb's gambol in field,
transformation of tillers toil into land's yield,
clear water shimmering with silvery fry,
clouds scudding along winds both low and high,
birds in nests incubating their breeds.
meandering brooks splashing through pine roots,
tossing and dancing of wild grass,
pristine deftness and aesthetic dexterity on a mould of brass,
whistle of brisk winds through pines,
brilliance in Evening Star's shine,
sprouting of seeds,
heavenly colors of natural beads,
are some vivid glimpses of his wild sequestered grace.
Yet, some of us, refuse to see His existence and trace.
The inherent beauty and peaceful serenity
of our nature, is His personal gift to us all;
both black and whites, rich and poor, big and small.
As in His eyes, there is just no discrimination,
since, each one of us, are His own extension and creation.
Remember, in things spiritual, heart is
better guide than mind.
Therefore, respect His gift and care for it if, you want Him
to remain benign and kind!

* * *

MY TRUTH

You're far more important to me than :-
Breath is for life,
aim is for strife,
Barman is for a pub,
bottom is for tub,
Ink for pen,
lion for den,
throttle for an air- machine,
a light source for a beam,
roof for a house,
burrow for a mouse,
milk for infant,
for a house owner his rent,
water for fish,
get up of a dish,
Starter for a race,
Metal tip for a shoe lace,
Umpire for match,
on a window, it's latch
on a tent, its centre hole.
For unemployed, his dole.
Without you, I am lost in an unknown land
Please tell me, where on earth in your wait, should I Stand!

* * *

MAGIC OF GOD

For me, you are in & around,
Up in heavens, deep in oceans beneath & above ground.
You re in everyone & everything everywhere.
With your benign mercies even, demons on our earth, you care.
Yours blessings know no bounds.
Without you, this life is worse than that of street dogs and hounds.
Some atheist profess, you're nowhere.
In times of need, they seek only you far and near.
For everyone, you hold the steering, brake and throttle.
Without a properly sealed cork, what good is any bottle?
If you wish, poorest of poor would taste the costliest cake,
if you turn your back, richest of all would beg for food
pleading and saying for God's sake.
You are omnipresent and mightiest of all.
The spirit behind a bat and ball.
Brightness of day and darkness at dead of night, so beautifully
     you make.
Your glory is evident in reflections of snow clad peaks
by day and night in still blue waters of a lake.
You're everyone's savior and protector.
All pervasive but, most elusive benefactor.

* * *

ALL ROUND ADVANCEMENT

I've watched, women fetching
water in pitchers from a common
village well, many times.
With a row of pitchers on their
head, they walk back
dancing and singing rhymes.
They tread along tracks,
slush and by-lanes,
sometimes, in sun and sometimes
    in rain.
Nothing happens to the row of
pitchers, neatly placed one on top
of the other, which are filled,
    right up to their brim.
These women are of all ages and
    both fat and trim
Most fascinating part is; not a
drop of water trickles down.
Right up to their houses, they're
absolutely dry including their head
    and gown.
I reckon that no matter what
they are talking 'n' doing, their
mind is tuned to maintain
pitcher's stability,
Past experience, of their subconscious
concentration, have given them now
    this ability.
They can go on like this
    any distance,
despite way side attraction and
    resistance.

I think that's exactly how
one should live this life.
Keep tuned to Him at all times from within and
put up all efforts to cope up with this worldly strife.
So that, we don't break pitchers
and get home absolutely wet.
Amidst materialism and worldly
chores, forgetting His blessings,
mercies and our debt.
This is, to my mind, very much practicable.
Perhaps, that's how, we could advance both materialistically and
spiritually while keeping all along our minds most stable.

* * *

THIRD EYE

All are blessed with Divine third eye.
That's how, there dwells in everyone that innate
power to sieve truth and a lie.
It's unique as, it's invisible and seated
    deep beneath forehead.
Closes for all times, once one's conscience is dead.
When it's fully open its unimaginable versatility and fidelity
    knows no bounds.
Astonishingly, besides viewing, it can perceive
    weakest of sounds.
Some listen to their inner rhythms and make its
    substantial use,
and thus, avoid falling prey to any cosmic ruse.
It sees objects beyond physical view
images are deep sharp and crystal clear like,
    on green grass, morning dew.
It's a port from where conscience emits lights
    of invisible frequency bands.
It's so powerful that, it can beam on anything
    beyond known lands.
Through it, innate goodness finds mute yet, very
    powerful expressions.
It can ward off in twinkling of an eye, all kinds
    of catastrophes and mental depressions.
Without investigation, it can differentiate
    between fact and fiction.
Impressions gathered through it, are nothing
but absolute pure logic and diction.
He has, through it, bestowed on all His own sights.
So that, man could understand, the interaction of
    both visible and invisible worldly lights.

Those, who constantly practice using it for other's good,
develop in due course, latent powers to hold
    any serpent by the hood.
Since, most people kill their conscience number of
    times each day,
third eye remains closed and that Divine telepathic
    ray doesn't find its way.
How about making right and apt use of His
    superb gift?
Your soul would automatically be upgraded
    and get that requisite lift.!

* * *

COULD YOU DO ME A FAVOUR?

Close to my end, could I have :-
    A glittering smile on my face
    Feeling of outright winner of the race.
    Your gracious and benign presence by my side,
    a truthful and honest heart with nothing to hide.
    Your life -size picture in front of my eyes,
    My speech without deceit, fraud and lies.
    Your name alone on my lip,
    My whole body in your divine, bliss full
        heavenly dip.
    Your personal benign invitation,
    self in coma of your reverential admiration.
    My own kith and kin wishing good bye without a tear,
    no devils and demons of this and that world, anywhere near.
        Flash-back of sweet memories of how well
        you cared for me, right from inception.
    A truthful expression of my thanks giving
        without any deception.
    My body engulfed in aura, halo and aroma
        of your light, fragrance, and musk.
    On those fateful last moments of my life's dusk.
    I don't think I' d been unjustified in my demands.
    For it, I'm prepared to accept throughout life,
        willingly, all your reprimands.

* * *

I'M BECAUSE OF YOU

Without your love,
    I' m a piece of an archive
    an abandoned beehive.
Without your nearness,
    I look like a duster without rubbing cloth,
    beneath light source, a wingless moth.
Without your touch,
    I'm sitting duck in front of a hunter,
    Amidst ponies and mules, a renowned punter.
Without your Caress.
    I'm not what I am,
    most ugly like a straight horned ram
Without Your charms.
    I'm like Dead Sea,
    like in winter, cup of ice cold tea.
Without Your presence,
    I'm a stranger in my own house,
    like amidst draught, a field mouse.
Without your company,
    I feel as if, I was a hunted fugitive;
        wanted dead or alive,
An aircraft pilot, unable to pull out of a nose dive.
    I'm, believe you me, because of you, my dear,
Without you, my helplessness is
worth a million scoff and jeer.
Your love, nearness, touch, caress, charms,
presence and company coax me to live on.
Otherwise, long time back, I' d have gone!

* * *

ONE WAY TICKET

Without Him, there's no chance of genuine peace.
There's no place on earth, where you could
    possibly get it on lease,
He can't attend to you as, there're
billions like you at any one time
How do you expect Him to care for you
when you indulge in all sorts of crime?
Your breath is synonymous of His benign
    and gracious existence.
What you do and not what you profess, is
    of greater significance.
In this great competition, you've to act
in a manner that, in all probability, He
    would like.
Therefore, you have to totally shake up
    your psyche.
He is with you when you speak truth,
impatiently and relentlessly help 'Have Nots'
Hence, you have to shun bad company and
    bad thoughts of all sorts.
After you have attracted His attention,
He would put you through many a test.
You've to go on despite cosmic delusions
    without losing fervor, zeal and zest.
When you go on doing good to others,
you'll never feel tired.
Then, your name, message and benevolence
will spread like wild jungle-fire.
Your life span is important if you realize
    it's worth.
Then alone, you could experience that
Divine happiness and peace on this very earth.

Between birth and death, you've been
given a life chance to prove your bona fides.
If you sincerely try, you'll always find
    Him by your side.
Don't waste any more breath and with
    full faith, repeat His name.
Otherwise, for wasting this unique chance.
all your excuses are more than lame.

* * *

DIVINE BLESSINGS

Listen to conscience which
    always gives messages divine.
Don't waste your life in counting
    only beads & dime.
Your soul seeks union with God
    as, it is His separated part,
but, you're dragging it miles away
by indulging in cruel & uncivilized
    deeds of all sort.
Your human form is his unique gift
& for your wandering soul the only chance.
Therefore, spare sometime for His company
    through meditation & trance,
If you help suffering humanity, you won't get
out of the materialistic race.
Remember, at the end of your life-race,
it alone, would turn out to be
    your saving grace.
So what, if you die a billionaire?
So what, if at that time, best of
    doctors were present to care?
Ultimate truth is that all your
materialistic possessions are left behind.
This wretched world would remember
you for sometimes only if, you're
    benevolent, humane & kind.
there was a sign board on a cemetery which read 'here
are many who once thought without
them this would come to an end'
Obviously, they somehow, completed
their life -span without a stitch or a mend.

For materialistic pleasures, everyone is
    in a sort of mad race.
So much so, that people don't have
time even to notice wrinkles on their face.
Death doesn't spare as, it comes to all.
Yet, there're a few to whom, it comes
only when, they wish & call.
By developing inner powers, you
could control even time.
In that wonderful stage, whole world would
get shrunk in one beautiful rhyme.
Therefore, seek to get His blessings
in order to experience unknown &
unfathomable pleasures.
With your concerted and concentrated efforts alone,
You could possess these divine treasures.

* * *

TRANSFORMATION

Amidst torrential rains, within me,
I experience a severe draught,
Amidst cheers & happiness, within me,
I carry a sad & dead heart.
My body cells seem to have
undergone a great chemical change.
My brain researches on
    subject's weird & strange.
Sea, sky & flowers don't enthuse
    & amuse me anymore.
Like, manhood of a customer,
    doesn't interest any whore.
Life itself, seems a long drawn
    affair & a big bore.
I'm as good as dead.
Everywhere, I carry a lifeless head.
Friends wonder what's wrong!
Why am I without a smile & song?
To me, life appears without any romance,
like, without music & dance.
With my realization and with added years to my age,
I've gone far away from my creator,
I've started hating myself
like friends hate a traitor.
My eye's focus is now fixed inside.
Exploring myths & mysteries
which, so elusively, within me hide.

* * *

STARS ARE FOR EVER

Each dawn & dusk is ushered in by morning & evening
    star,
so is, each life spark.
Morning star of life is mother, in whose womb,
life finds an attire.
Evening star is own increment;
(In Hindu religion; the last rites are performed by the eldest son,)
who, ceremoniously
    brings an end to this lifelong satire.
There are some dusks & dawns when skies aren't clear.
The usherer too, in life, sometimes, isn't in sight or
    become queer.
Sometimes, these stars are unusually bright,
    heralding a promising day & night.
Similarly, usher of life sometimes, is
    unusually lovable & sweet.
& help make life span enjoyable & rather neat.
Life gets ushered in any-where in this world in
    the same known way.
Morning & evening stars anywhere in this world, are
    Synonymous of each clear day.
Stars don't wither away; in fact, are continuously aglow
    With the same intensity.
So is the soul, which, wanders in various attires
    With the same propensity.
With each dress, soul gets spiritually either upgraded
    Or degraded.

Consequently, the halo around her either gets
  brighter or faded.
In this regard, selfless & kind acts for other suffering souls
alone, could help.
Remember, each such act is life's real achievement by itself!

* * *

IT'S NOT ALL THAT DIFFICULT

God resides inside
where, dazzling cosmic lights hide.
To realize His presence, you need to have
    a sincere desire.
Undeviating, persistence in inner investigation
    would reveal Him oh, my sire!
Otherwise, you'll remain bound life-long with
bad habits & fetters of ignorance,
& hence anxious, worried & tense.
Our heart has to conceive of Him as
    life's highest necessity,
& then, with utmost dedication, one can
    realize that self itself is Divinity.
Search lights of inner super consciousness can
show galaxies beyond the realm if imagination.
Spiritual ecstasy can be experienced with meditation.
Actually, if you have the perception, you'll see Him everywhere
& therefore, in you, He would take a very personal care.
Mere prosperity & Gracious living isn't enough,
without discipline & control on body & mind,
    Life is bound to be tough.
An ardent spiritual seeker invariably finds, Him.
Whereas one, who whiles away time & shabbily playing
with life, is bound to have spirits low & dim.
The delusive powers of materialism, divert one's
awareness from spirit to matter.
Truth & reality then, scatter.

If, you choose the life that leads to Him,
real eternal happiness would seize you
   right up to your brim.
He would, then throb Divine wisdom in your
mind & real joy in heart.
You would sail through straight, without
worries & fears like, a dart.

* * *

BEST INSURANCE

Niggling doubts of days ahead.
generally cause a heavy head.
What good is dying before being actually dead!
What good is in sighing unless the account balance is in red!
Your hopes & fears are your own brain -child.
Given too much vent, mind goes berserk & wild.
To redeem any suffering & torture, have insurance with God.
Pay up the premium regularly from the real wealth stored up in
your heart & mind in the name of your lord.
To begin with, remember Him off & on
& experience your self-created fears gone.
Then onwards, invest in His name every breath
until, your seemingly physical death.
His insurance would cover not only body but,
      your soul.
Payment of premiums won't make you experience
      a big drain or a heavy toll.
Also, your soul would remain under insurance
cover till eternity.
As hereafter, you would have become part &
      parcel of His own fraternity.
Obviously, materialistic policies don't provide
us a good choice.
That's why, we stand absolutely aloof in this
world without hearing His own voice!
You need to seek insurance cover with
both intellect & intelligence.
Your actions life-long then, would be
marked with forbearance, fortitude & diligence!

Remember, helping hands are better than praying lips.
This insurance would ensure for thee life long
heavenly dips!
Be wise & invest without wasting any more time.
Otherwise, be prepared to suffer unknown privations just for a rhyme!
People left behind, won't remember you
for what all you gathered.
But, by how much you scattered!

* * *

REALISM

LIFE

It's an uncontrolled dream
    abruptly ends.
It's a mountain of smoke
    with indistinguishable & unpredictable bends.
You care for your body so much
    and to satisfy it, materialistic pleasures
    you search.
At the fag-end, the same leaves you in lurch.
Flesh and bones are only a cage for your soul.
Its up liftment alone, should therefore, be your only goal.
You set your heart on unreal and mortal things.
    and wasted a fair chance.
Live with Him every moment in meditation and trance.
How's your life different from that of an ant who
    also, lives full life cycle and dies?
If you, didn't see Him everywhere and lived on white lies!
Remember Him, Sing His praises and do what He says.
For achievement of 'Moksha'[12] there are no other ways.
Billions of souls in various attires are wandering
    in dark on the face of our earth.
Remember, very few finally get free from the cycle of birth
and rebirth.
Where is the harm in sincerely trying?
Otherwise, you came crying, cried through life
    and will also, end up crying.
Like morning stars start receding into oblivion,
    so does life spark,
Its cage then appears like fungus eaten tree bark.
Issue of life and death is decided by a breath tender.
    Remember, death keeps no calendar!

* * *

A UNIQUE MESSAGE

It was majestic, enchanting, one of the lovely
    spring mornings.
Nature was in its best and it impelled my heart
glue on my surroundings.
When I beheld, bewitching sun rays dancing on dew over
    lush green grass,
thousands of butterflies acrobating over flowers en masse.
Peacocks in their fascinating dance,
I thought nature in its pristine beauty endowed on me
a unique chance.
When I heard sweet hum of bees and chirping birds,
    love notes of cuckoo & of nightingale,
I realized Nature's bounty, grandeur and splendor
    wasn't a mere tale.
I felt rejuvenating strokes of pure, fresh
    and musky breeze,
Strangely enough, I was bereft of worries and
    felt absolutely at ease.
Looked around most peacefully to feast eyes with
    nature's magnanimity.
My expression certainly lacked apt words to describe
    it's pristine beauty and serenity.
When I beheld thousands of flowers in unique blend
of colors and smilingly giving hearty invitation.
I reckoned Nature had given color and shape to
    even its smallest of creation.
Tranquility, serenity and magnanimity were integral
    to Nature's charm.

No wonder, the right minded one's, in its benign
      vicinity remained always calm,
Nature gave us the message of sense of sharing,
      love and peace.
But, man was ever busy in drawing artificial lines
      of caste and creed.
Instead of communicating Nature's benign message
      from one to another,
He seemed hell bent to destroy it, who nurtured
      him like a mother.
Now, he plans, prepares and boasts of a win
      even in a nuclear war.
His pseudo wisdom prompts him to think that
his mite if not more than that of his creator
      is definitely at par.
He dubs the logical analysis of what will
      follow nuclear holocaust as dubious.
His mind in zest of materialistic howlers, had
      become more than vicious.
Undoubtedly, experience is the other name that
      one gives to one's mistakes.
Wise is he who, implements lessons that he makes.
If unprecedented devastation and untold human
sufferings at Hiroshima & Nagasaki is our
      folly and failure,
It's time we let the conscience rule us rather
than our egoistic and sentimental heart and
      sincerely search a cure.
Crying need of the hour is to sweep the
filth of our mind with the broom of wisdom,
and help make our planet an abode of peace and
      God's own kingdom.
Could, anyone have a say when and where to take birth!

Yet, we're inimical to one another for our parentage, religion
nationality, caste and creed on the face of our common earth.
God created one earth, one man, one woman and beautiful
nature to look after their need.
Alas! man : the most advanced and civilized of all creations,
drew maps and divided self in pseudo bondages of religion,
color and creed.
When will man stop fooling with nature?
When will be understand amidst the galaxy of nature his own
stature?
When will years go by without children dying of hunger and
starvation?
When will he make their future absolutely safe and revere them
as God's own manifestation?
When will 'Haves' stop imposing their brutal will on the 'Have
Nots'?
When will he give due priority to human dignity in his words and
deeds of all sorts?
When will people stop their struggle either to make our world
red or safe for democracy?
When will rich let the poor have square meals and stop living
life of hypocrisy?
When will man use his servants; wisdom and atom for peace,
progress and prosperity of all mankind?
I pray for such a blessed time soon enough lest,
With his satanic, savage and demon-like deeds, he leaves
life-less, brutally shaken and dead earth behind!

* * *

THE MOST USELESS OF ALL

Man is the most useless animal;
His skin in not worth shoes.
His flesh, if given choice, carnivorous
don't choose.
His bones aren't good for any use.
Bone marrow even ants refuse.
But, this useless animal is extremely cunning,
trades fellow human's organs and keeps life running
He'll sell blood at premium and exploit situation.
He'll mar other's happiness for his own recreation.
With his gift of brain, he considers himself superior than
all other life forms.
To meet his ends, creates for fellow beings,
tempests and storms.
His cunningness makes him feel very proud.
His curses and abuses on poor and innocent hapless are rather loud.
Rich treat poor as their subject.
In the process of extracting the last blood out of the poor,
whatever they may do, consider it justified and correct
He forgets that sighs and curses of a hapless are worse
than any known devastating fire.
What a pity, seemingly more civilized
Out of the lot, are heartless and liar.
When will he understand his rightful role?
There seems no way as, he's hell bent to sell his soul.

* * *

TWO GREAT REALITIES

Birth and death are only two realities
and rest all a big crap.
Birth is like waking up at dawn
And death an unending eternal nap.
In between the two realities, lies a complete life story.
Alas! almost everyone lives amidst
yet, doesn't recognize His benign glory.
all kinds of comforts and pleasures,
he gives, straight in one's lap,
makes one wear many a crown and cap.
Although, He is in and around
and His blessings know no bound.
Yet, one never thinks of Him and keeps Him so far away.
That's exactly where, the whole problem lay.
Life without Him, is a sheer experience of suffocation and pain.
One could feel unfathomable pleasures and solace by just being
humane.
You lose nothing by being a gentleman and kind
whereas, you lose every thing
when, a hapless suffers before you & you turn blind.
No one can hold time as it keeps ticking on.
Similarly, no one can hold sand in the palm grip
as, it keeps slipping down.
Making this gap between birth and death
Charming, is in one's own hand.
Your deeds alone can make your story remarkably grand.

* * *

PASSENGER

I entrained for predetermined destination
and entrusted my life in the hands of a driver, unknown.
Never pondered about his skills and competence,
or gave vent to moan or groan.
I'd a compartment and seat number allotted to me
and therefore, my environment wasn't of my choice.
I'd to accept them without making fuss or a noise.
I came across people of all sorts;
some close and some far.
To some. Even, I talked freely without any bar.
Some, I found friendly and compatible
and from some, I kept distance.
In the company of some, time flew and
I, unknowingly got closer to my destination.
Some, came in en route and got down.
Some, were there when I boarded and
were destined for a further ahead town.
Some, were rich, some not so rich and some, poor,
some, were aimless travelers and some,
on private or official tour.
Some, were healthy and cheerful,
some, with unhealthy mind and looked fearful.
Passengers of all sorts were going on the same track
and getting closer to their destinations every second.
For some, thought occupied them so much
that they reached destinations before they could reckon.
Track for all, was sometimes
straight and sometimes took a curve.
Some, always kept their cool and
some, lost their nerve.

For some, it was a happy journey
and for some, a big bore.
Some, awaited destination with forbearance and patience
And some, awaited impatiently at the door.
It went over brooks and rivers.
Some, felt pleased and some had quivers.
Sometimes, the scenery around was a feast to the eye,
and sometimes, hands spontaneously went up
waving good bye to passers-by.
The driver drove sometimes fast and sometimes slow.
Passengers had no say whatsoever,
and could do nothing but bow.
Train while on move, made sounds
Sometimes jarring and sometimes fascinating,
Thus, some shrieked and for some, it was rejuvenating.
Aren't all of us passengers in this life train?
We don't realize how fast are we moving
and that's surely our biggest bane!
Undoubtedly all of us will
reach our respective destinations.
Some with a smile on face and some in pain.
Some in high spirits and some, with their spirits down in the drain.
Some, sane and some, absolutely insane.
He could endow us all with
inner vision to consider this journey as if, a great celebration.
While we could gladly share our joys with all & ensure
smile on everyone around without any hesitation!

* * *

TOGETHER, WE SUSTAIN LIFE

My wait at last, ended and I smilingly sprouted.
Nectar of heavenly dew nurtured my hood,
Amidst rejuvenating sun, peaceful moon and
pure strokes of breeze, I stood.
In abundance of nature's love, I attained a huge form.
Soon, I was strong enough to brave the vagaries of nature
and triumphed many a gale and storm.
When a hot and red sun was right on top,
travelers pointed towards me as a cool and shady spot.
Birds of all sorts as if, loved my company,
fluttered their wings, sang songs and
merrily chirped nesting their young ones upon me.
Even the wild bee, collected enormous nectar and honey.
My joy knew no bounds when, I saw a
tired traveler resting peacefully in my lap,
I thought except love, and just love,
rest was all crap.
Even whistling winds
through me, sounded like an ecological jazz.
while I got tossed all over.
I desired to live long only to help other fellow living beings
was unaware that someone nearby mutely
admired timber and dead fire-wood in me
On that fateful night, I saw him advancing
towards me holding obnoxious tools with determined steps.
Wish I could run or plead in his language to be out of his webs!
With every stroke of his brutal axe, I cried in solitude.
Pleading mercies in my language, Alas! unknown and inaudible.
Instead, he was ruthless, pitiless
and remorseless in all its magnitude.

He went on unabated and unmindful of
how much I had done for him,
Perhaps he couldn't care less as his money was sure only,
when, he reached the other end of my rim.
Birds and bees had abandoned me in a great sorrow
knowing what was in store.
Here was this wretched man determined to down me for sure.
I couldn't bear any more and fell with a
great thud and there was an earth rumble.
Now that, I was to be dead, I fell with all my dead weight
on that heartless, brutal and savage without a fumble.
Both of us, now, lay motionless and dead;
Me, with his barbaric attack and he,
in retaliation, under my tread.
Strange enough, both of us were part of the same pyre.
Both of us, got consumed in one big fire.
Wish we'd lived together hand in hand a bit longer!
I would have certainly endeavored to make his life on earth
richer and stronger.
Remember, as long as I live, you will.
Without me, you're like a bald and barren hill;
withering and eroding day in and day out.
Rest assured, it's nothing but, self destruction
and complete rout.

* * *

PLAIN SPEAKING

Since your inception, I suffer your weight benign.
A day will dawn, when you suffer mine.
Promptly you remove an ant from your
body, even while in sleep.
Then, all sorts of insects, all over your body
without any bother, shall crawl and creep.
They'll feast on you merrily in thousands
and spare only your hollow and tasteless bones.
I'll then, consume you under my weight
and heat without inviting any moan or groan.
I am the chief witness to this grim reality
since countless years.
If you believe in it, I'm certain you'll
save all your tears.
With your satanic and demon-like deeds,
you get fatter and heavier upon me and you really tire.
No doubt. on that fateful day, I'll witness
your sufferings and privations, oh! my sire.
To me, all rich and poor, famous and insignificant
come over the same way.
All your near and dear ones return you to me
for eternal peace; so do all say.
As, it is beyond your powers to decide
where to emerge for His life drama.
So is, beyond your powers to decide piece of six feet
upon me, after that abrupt and rude trauma.
If you keep this grim reality and absolute truth,
while you live, in mind.

I'm sure you'll do good and continue to live amidst
memories of those left behind.
I'm earth; your planetary abode, where you experience
false heaven and hell and earn a place
in eternal heaven or hell by your deeds.
I wonder, after knowing this truth, would you
still keep counting only your beads!

* * *

SILENT SPECTATOR

When I show up, valley mists rise
& all nocturnal seek a hide.
Birds flutter wings and sing my praise.
My devotees offer me river water and fix through it their gaze.
Fishes come up as if, to have my glimpse
and dance out of pool or river at random
Rooster go on calling unabated to welcome me in tandem.
Elders throng temples and seek blessings from
their deities for the day.
Dew over grass, sparkles like heavenly gems &
turn onlooker's mood optimistic and gay.
Leaves move majestically with refreshing breeze
in search of my ray.
Some of you, somewhere, seeing me, exclaim
and greet each other jubilantly saying, what
a bright sunny day!
With my advent, some of you walk and run but,
some adamant and incorrigible amidst you, stir up only
when, I'm right on top of the nose and disturb your fun.
Then onwards, almost everyone gets into a mad race.
To me, all of you, are in just a wild goose chase.
Everyone rushes to the place of his business,
also, the beggar
Somewhere, a soldier under the shelter, cleanse
his gun & dagger
Mothers remind their young ones to return
home before sun is down.
Bread winners under my nose, remain only busy in
collecting their Pound.

From dawn to dusk, you feel me far and near.
I'm a silent witness to your joy, sweat and tear.
I bring light in your life
Have you ever pondered how to make it
a meaningful strife?
I attempt to remind you at dusk my annoyance
at your ways and means, through my red face.
You purposely refuse to get my message lest,
you lose your self-created materialistic race!
Days go by and you see me every day.
When will you look inwards and turn your
life really joyous and gay?
If you ever at the end of the day, pondered
in retrospect what you did!
I promise you to help remove the
heavenly pitcher's lid.

* * *

NAKED TRUTH

I was in my tender years.
Life was full of smiles and cheers.
God had been kind to bestow upon me
happiness and satisfaction.
I was unaware of human misery, sufferings and
complex social interaction.
One fine morning, I heard crying and wailing sounds;
I was told, the rich man, who lived next door,
had breathed his last and his kith and kin.
made preparations for cremation grounds.
I hadn't seen a dead and had no idea on
his last voyage.
So, I sneaked out and joined the dead man's entourage.
What I saw, couldn't believe,
hard realities of life were too harsh for me to
perceive.
His near and dear ones had robbed him off
his body gold and rich clothes that he
always wore,
Some around him, shed crocodile tears, &
some mutely described him an eye sore.
The man who, once boasted of guiding the nation's destiny,
lay motionless, frozen and pale.
His life for associates was now, a mere tale.
His wealth and riches couldn't buy him
even one more breath.
I wondered why, for such a cosmic delusion,
he remained engrossed until his death.
People told his last moments were sad and full of gloom
since, he couldn't bear the pangs of separation
from his wealth, riches and fortune.

He rested on a strange cot of bamboo poles
and cross bars and
there're no mattresses, cushions and sheets in sight.
I'm sure, his body, on this rude and crude
treatment, must had cried in solitude on his plight.
For the first time, he got out of his mansion
in a strange gait;
During his life, he was either carried in chauffeur
driven limousines or travelled distances by air,
but, today, his kith and kin customarily were
to shoulder his dead weight.
Females broke pitcher half way and returned
no more grief stricken.
Back home, they got busy as usual, with their kids and kitchen.
The rest of the relatives meanwhile, took him
to cremation grounds in a record breaking time,
where, a pundit[13], as a matter of routine and drill,
awaited to commence voicing last ritual rhyme.
Dead was ordered to be placed on sandal wood pyre,
amidst rich smells of fragrances,
& then his eldest son showed him fire.
Soon, fire rose high towards sky and consumed
his flesh and bone.
His corporate remains kissed its fury and ferocity without a groan.
While the eldest son went around,
crowd and the Pundit awaited impatiently to
hear the skull bursting sound.
No one could leave the site without hearing that,
even if the rest of the body had vanished in glow.
The eldest one, equally impatient at last, delivered
a hard stick-blow.
The dead man in his life must have sacrificed
many a comfort and pleasure for his son.

I'm sure he was unaware that he would get
this treatment in return.
crowd heard much awaited sound and priest
announced the end of ceremony.
Mourners strangely enough, chatted on their way
back about business, politics and tastes of nectar
and honey.
No one talked about the grim reality and
stark naked truth that man came penniless
and went away without a penny.
Because, the cosmic delusions of the materialistic world
were so strong and so many.
Soon, sons and daughters filed law suits
to usurp his left over property,
till they breathed their last, the rich man's fortune
remained a perpetual source of their spiritual poverty.
Isn't struggle for money, power, riches and fortune
a wasteful activity?
Only service before self reinforced spiritual strength
& meaningful life's longevity!

* * *

UNLUCKY ONES

Night was pitch dark, cold and the clock
struck midnight.
People's dream fantasies behind closed doors were
in their wild flight.
Street dog's wailing, only, broke the uncanny silence,
even for lone-walker, night was unusually tense.
Bone-chilling wind kept even thieves in doors.
Only mice were having a gala time in their
respective stores.
Not far away, there sat strange fellows
beating Bongos and singing song.
Head of their clan called it a day, which was unusually long.
During his life, he danced in many a house
when babe was born,
His presence was considered good omen and joyful parents
happily gave in return, rupee and corn.
Her songs, claps and mannerism was unique.
For males, his sight amusing and females refused
to consider her one of their clique.
Members of his clan awaited the darkest and
dense hour of the night.
When, the roads and streets would be dead and
not a soul in sight.
They began to perform last rites in a strange way;
House was fully lit, doors ajar and mood all around gay,
They pulled him by his hair and arms while
her body dragged along the road all the way,
everyone of his clan shoed her one by one
on that fateful day.

They asked him, while shoeing, only one question;
Will you ever in this form come again or now so say?'
Whatever remained of her body after such a long drag and
shoeing, was shown fire.
Everyone, rejoiced the fact that now, one more
soul shan't ever get eunuch's attire.
Our pseudo humane society forced these unlucky ones
to live in segregation.
The hermaphrodite's life and death no doubt was
an utter degradation.
Thank Him for He didn't send you here as one.
With His grace, you are some body's daughter or son.
If He wished, what would hapless like you would have done!
Except, pray that once again in that human form
you shouldn't come!

* * *

I'M THE TIME

I vividly remember how this universe came into being.
I clearly recollect how sun and it's family around it
commenced spinning.
Moments of introduction of life spark into protozoa
on your beautiful earth, are more than fresh in my mind.
I can recount the currents of evolution
which saw through the same life spark into
8.4 million forms and kind.
I've witnessed the first ever love enacted by human form.
Do you know, you're a product of atomic fusion of
human heat and emotional storm?
I have seen you waging wars and creating your history.
So called mysterious ways of yours, for me, aren't any mystery.
I unfold myself and make you realize the truth.
I'm a great healer and make you
forget even a bloody tooth.
I am the greatest of all and from me nothing is hidden.
Great man-made upheavals over the annals of your history
are like blood stains on my white linen.
I can't wash them even if, I try,
They're the foot prints on mud
of an incorrigible one and sly.
You can't fathom my mite.
No one could, can and would ever arrest my flight.
If, I let you know what is in store,
life for you, will become stand still and a great bore.
I've known you as a nasty creature.
You don't take stock of me
just because, I' am silent preacher.
I'm a reality with you and with
everyone else around.

Under various impulses, various needs and wants
in your mind, gather ground.
If, I bestow upon you good times,
you call yourself lucky and sing it away in rhymes.
If, I get tough with you and unfold suffering,
You rebuke your fate and forget even mimicking.
I'm teaching you every moment if ever, in me, you stare!
Learn it or not, I've taught myself by now
not to get bothered and unduly care.
I've left it to you and
to your inner wisdom,
since, you stand today on the cross roads of preservation
or destruction of your kingdom.
Like it or not, your doings, I'll narrate to those living beings
who, once again appear, may be innumerable years from now.
To my unknown silent self, you have no alternative but to bow.
Your whole life is, what I Unfold
If you respect me, I'll turn anything you touch
into pure Gold!

* * *

LIFE DRAMA

It's an unending drama;
A perfect synthesis of pathos, melancholy,
gregariousness and trauma.
All play important roles as stage actors.
scene, role, type of character, timings, stage settings
are some of the uncontrolled tangible factors.
Entry on to stage is almost similar
but, very familiar.
Some, expect new actor's arrival and await impatiently.
Some, as a matter of routine, watch the beginning silently.
While some, greet each other jubilantly.
What a reception; no clapping, and no ovations.
New one is hung upside down.
& then, some professional gives a whack on his bottoms
In a strange town.
The very first noise under dazzling artificial lights,
is a protest in the familiar form of loud shriek.
It spontaneously draws smiles on all around
and all heave thankfully a sigh of relief.
Then onwards, under unknown director, on various stage
Settings, actor plays his destined part & performs many a character role
under various environment of all sort.
The quality of acting and role
influence both spectators and co-actors
On this enormously big stage, billions of actors
perform well knit & coordinated roles as different characters.
After the performance, all leave the stage
in a well known common style, in this ever running show.
New actors continuously enter and old ones leave,
as if, in a row.

Some, go unnoticed and some, leave permanent and
indelible imprint on many an onlooker.
To some, audience respects with standing ovation.
and for the disappearance of some, they thank the director.
Some, through their part, make spectators happy
and some make them cry.
Some, play double roles and some fraudulently short cuts try.
Some, with practice, get more matured in the art
and during the drama itself, become celebrities.
While some, with passage of time, invite only pities.
The director maintains somehow, a judicious balance
between comedy and tragedy throughout the play.
I suppose that's how interest of both actors and spectators
in it, stay!
Right kind of role, right timings, right stage setting, right
type of audience and right kind of promptings
from behind the stage, only a few lucky ones, get.
However, the whole drama is speculative and anyone's guess.
Exactly, like the number of fish in a fisherman's net.

* * *

JUST REMEMBER!

All those, who came this way,
have gone back only one way;
Body rests on same throne and with same thread
just like, a stone or heap of lead.
In this regard, nobody ever had any say
Yet, out of billions there are just a few
who, at that juncture, were really happy & gay.
There is always that righteous and divine ray.
but, alas! all of us, merrily keep groping in dark & therefore,
isn't it time to take stock of things around
without wasting yet another day?
Otherwise, remember, unaffordable price
you'll have to pay.
It's a fact that as one is never too late.
All of us possess that innate goodness,
the practice of which, will make us really great.
No one has carried anything from here ever.
Therefore, how about at the very outset,
stop fooling around and being too clever!
Richest of all, generally, have lived spiritually
the most poor man's life.
Only, at the end of the road, did they realize
how wasteful had been their life-long strife?
Your riches and fortunes, remember,
never make you really rich.
Pseudo materialistic fascinations and attractions,
drag you more and more in a hellish ditch.
More you get sucked in, more darkness
in seemingly glittering environments around, prevails.

Near your end you feel just like, a helpless sailor
in deep stormy sea, without his sails.
You'll do a lot of good to self, if you shun egoism
and remain human at all times.
How about using for suffering humanity your dimes?
Otherwise, remember, you are a criminal in His eyes
and will be punished here and hereafter
for all your known and unknown crimes.
just remember!

* * *

JUST A MATTER OF TIME

The journey from Cradle to coffin
is just a matter of time.
There are times when, own reflections prompt one
no end of oneself.
There are times when the same are horrid and dreadful,
It's just a matter of time.
There are times when, one feels on top of the world
and scoffs at others.
There are times when, the same haplessly lingers on
and his days look like years.
There are times when one is agile, nimble and quick.
Also, there are times when, own feet refuse to click;
It's just a matter of time.
There are times when, one ridicules God and hurls curses.
Yet, there are times when, staunch atheists invoke Him
and beg his mercies;
It's just a matter of time.
There are times when one considers self no less
than Mohammed Ali.
There are also times, when physical strength
invokes self-pity;
It's just a matter of time
There are times when me, I, and My only dominate one's speech.
There are times when he can't even shriek;
It's just a matter of time.
There are times when, one sermons ways to success.
Yet, at the fag-end finds whole life in a veritable mess,
It's just a matter of time.

There are times when, one feels confident of riding on
the whole world.
Yet at another, feels tame, & helpless timid as a wingless bird;
It's just a matter of time.
The life of an infant and that of an old ager
are similar in many ways.
One wonders, how quickly vanished one's days!
This realization is just a matter of time.
Amassing wealth through ill means make one feel.
clever and smart.
Mental agony and torture of keeping property
intact, make one feel like, a dummy cart.
It's just a matter of time.
Since, this time can't be quantified as a thumb rule.
why slog in ignorance and die the
death of a mountain mule?
A blind, orphan, deaf & dumb, retarded and leper
by birth are all His creation.
They certainly deserve love and honorable affiliation.
Just devote some time for them daily and
see for yourself, how good you feel!
Reinforce your goodness through actions and then, all dark and
evil spirits around you will bow and kneel.

* * *

TEARS AND TEARS ALL THE WAY

Tears are expressions of my emotion,
    That of sorrow and joy
That's how I'm so different from a toy.
Like clouds commune with parched earth
    beneath with their tears,
Spontaneous welled up eyes sometimes,
    symbolize my latent fears.
Your tears on my lips and mine on your lips,
For our inseparable souls, are like heavenly dips.
These droplets even out the turbulence of my mind.
Fears, anxieties and emotional stresses
    come under a draconic grind.
Salinity in them is uniquely sweet.
Rate of their flow downwards follow
    a strange rhythm and beat.
Tears are there in every human's eyes.
Without shedding them, believe me,
    no one in this world, anywhere, dies.
They're true replicas of feelings of heart.
Human eyes and innocent tears can't be kept apart.
Strangely enough, their chemistry is different
    from one set of circumstance to another.
Analogous to the difference even in
    uni-ovular twin brothers.
It is a byproduct of emotional reactions
    beneath deep recesses of mind.
They've the power to turn a
    savage into a kind.
These pearls are both artificial and natural.

Without them, this life drama, will be intriguing,
    undoubtedly, not so enchanting and dismal.
Blessed are ones who shed tears of joy and ecstasy.
Blessed are ones who don't, as they, respect.
    the inner voice of prophecy.
When you shed tears, you shed a million ton load.
Just make sure somehow, that you don't do it
    at the end of the road.
The slogan of 'tears for others and not for self.'
for this volatile, turbulent and turmoiled
    world society, perhaps, only could help!

* * *

REALITIES OF LIFE

Defenses which lack depth, easily crumble,
people who lack depth, always grumble.
Those, who lack character, have personal defenses
only skin deep.
Those, who listen to their conscience, rich dividends reap.
Those, who talk aloud, generally lack guts
Those, who live in palaces, must also know
how to do so in huts.
Those, who wield powers and become proud,
turn deaf towards the inner massage of humility and kindness,
even when, it is clear and loud.
Generally, wander aimlessly like, a dry cloud
and eventually, suffer a great traumatic rout.
I don't know why, after acquiring riches
through dishonest means, man forgets that
he still had two legs!
Since, he misuses and abuses these riches
for self and near 'n' dear ones, that, in the end,
he only begs.
After accumulating riches, do something
that may, make you feel really rich.
Remember, even in a fair game of cricket,
deliveries are penalized which, aren't well on the pitch
At the fag-end, those, whom you gave everything in life,
also, ditch.
You'll be really wise if, in time, you mend and stitch.

* * *

A BEAUTIFUL BEGINNING OF A TRAGIC END

The old is an infant & infant an old;
One comes out of infernal mother's womb fire.
The other, awaits to kiss the fury of his pyre.
One has just come and the other about to go.
One had a long drama ahead and the other
has almost finished his show.
One cries for, the other remembers and invokes
from heaven his mother.
No wonder, both remain unusually drawn to each other.
Infant is most peaceful on mother's breast.
Old is just fed up with prolonged rest.
Infant cries and laughs in the same breath, so does the old;
remembering, his good and bad deeds.
Others have to help both for their basic needs.
Infant knows not what's in store!
Old knows not, how many vicious cycles of birth more!
Infant chuckles and kicks at her mother's sight
Old bent with age, and head oscillating,
can't even cry at his plight.
New born speaks language unknown.
Old wants to plead with God. But his words
deep behind lips, drone.
Infant is like Ganges at its source.
Old, like it is, at the end of its course.
Child's face radiates innocence.
An old's terse, callous and tense.
Infant invites spontaneous love and affections.
The old remains drawn in his own reflections.
Does infant know that his years will lead him into infancy?

Old actually welcomes moments, which will
end his derangement and frenzy.
Relatives pick up infant and happily throw them up in air.
whereas, old suspiciously views his relatives' care.
Materialistic delusions and infant's ever growing senses
soon start corresponding.
Old's senses to these totally stop responding.
Infant on birth, yells as a protest to dazzling
artificial lights.
Old also, yells at the time of death with fear of
glimpses of weird after flights.
Infant can either get into or get out of the cycle of
rebirth and has a fair chance.
Old intricately webbed in cosmic delusion, is amidst
materialistic trance.
Both symbolize life;
One pure and fresh to go through
rigors of life here.
The other, pure and fresh to go through
rigors of life there.

* * *

WHERE DO YOU STAND?

Some of you, molest and rape,
you're worse than an ape.
Some of you, laugh when others cry,
your greedy eyes keep on other's women & wealth pry.
Some of you, think yourself smart and witty,
when you lie.
Waste food, when your neighbors out of sheer
starvation and hunger, die.
Some of you, rob innocent and plunder.
Are you the most civilized creature, I, wonder?
Some of you, live on other's toil life long,
and then, amidst society, pose like a monk,
& won't think twice before selling their honor for a song,
Some of you, terrorize and kill innocent and hapless,
the beast in them is most coward and can't withstand
any stress.
It's because of them, the life of a peace lover has
turned a veritable mess.
Some of you, regard immoral as moral and
twist the law abiding citizen's arms.
deceit simpletons by money power and apparent charms.
It's a unique mixture of some good and some bad,
some very intelligent, some mediocre
and some mad.
Some helpful, some callous and some always busy
causing nuisance.
Somehow, He has managed to maintain a terrific equilibrium in
essence.

In this Kalyug[14], these very people seem to be having a
royal ball.
Sure, they'll be tormented beyond imagination when they
get their final call.
I don't know if You exist, where and in what form
and know what's happening on your earth!
If You do, you won't let anyone kill any innocent
and destroy other's hearth.
Why don't You send Nanak, Gandhi and Mother Teresa
in every home?
I suppose You don't want to lose charm of this
big drama in Your omni-dome!
Good people shall have to go on doing good
regardless of privations, persecutions and
provocation.
Their lives undoubtedly then, shall kindle more goodness.
without any fear of divine retribution.

* * *

DEVIL'S DAY

Great seas will reign snow clad mountain peaks.
all human's flesh held in great vulture's beaks.
Underground creepers will twine around birds.
all carnivores in fear-stricken herds.
All green will get engulfed in sky fires.
In all cemeteries, a grand feast for all devils and liars.
Heat beneath will puff out its core and cause.
a great emulsification.
Planet disintegrating while heading towards
an unknown destination.
Earth's interior will be brighter than sun and
exterior plunged in mysteriously dreadful dark.
Hitherto, earth full of life, without a live spark.
Devil's amongst us are so powerful that they can undo
what nature's evolution has achieved over billions of years
in the twinkling of an eye.
Those, who hold push buttons, must know that, they'll too
in a split second, die.
It's the collective responsibility of whole humanity
to choose their leaders without devil finger tips.
Only those, who could use instead,
their Divine tongue and lips!

* * *

HER FACES

She has many a name;
Mother, sister, girl friend, wife, mother-in-law
daughter, are all manifestations of the same.
They say with all these attires in Eden's Garden, She came.
As a mother, she is compassionate, gracious and kind,
no wonders, every great man has known or unknown great
mother behind.
She proves her total superiority in this field without a
man's plead.
Since, it's universally known, men can't bear children
and breast feed.
Sisters enrich childhood and make you-feel brotherly.
Brother's learn to take care, voice, concern and shoulder
responsibility.
Girl friend, soothes your vibrant nerves and makes
you feel proud of association.
That's how an adolescent comes of age having learnt the
art of persuasion.
Heart-throb, sweet honey are youthful
expressions of love in carefree days.
Dramatic metamorphosis from adolescence to manhood
intricate with females, is why, a plot of many plays.
She enters in your life as a solemnly declared wife.
make you learn to love, hate-'n'-love and cope up with strife.
For some, it's smooth sail over rough seas and tide,
Yet, for some, bickering, frustrations and spells
of depressions are worth a hide.
For her man's blissful and peaceful life, she
lends a helping hand.
But, cruel and passionate man is ever busy
in raising through her, members of his band.

For some, her presence as mother-in-law, makes
them feel slave, oppressed and down trodden.
Her words hit you like darts draped in treated cotton.
Both sexes dread her and avoid her as much as they could.
Because, she has an uncanny knack of getting misunderstood.
The cruel society compels some to prostitute
and bestows upon her privations of a great multitude.
She responds to lust and pleasure seekers for coins,.
people find her an outlet for taking out water of their chest through groins.
Man had been cunning and clever over years;
assigned her a veil and four walls of his house
basically, to scare away his fears
In orthodox societies, she had been perennially
swallowing their tears.
Given a chance, she can prove equal if not better,
in many a field.
He's fast losing his self- created aura of pseudo-intellect
and masculine shield.
Man, intrigued with egoism and male chauvinism
has refused to learn her chemistry.
Doesn't realize that, she is a perfect, flawless
example of His artistry.
History of man bears testimony to a hard reality;
She'd been in some form behind all wars.
brutal killings, betrayals and cruelty.
If man desires real peace, he has to invest,
in the shape of equal status to her, love and respect.
Besides this, there seems no other way,
with 'Women's Lib' gearing up momentum,
man seemed to be heading for his doom's day.

* * *

WHAT A PITY!

These birds are more sensible as,
they don't divide their environment
for a particular breed.
These flowers are far more civilized
as they offer fragrance and aroma
irrespective of your caste and creed.
Fish is free of any artificial barriers.
Honey bees kiss and love all kinds of flowers and for nectar & honey,
become, in return, their pollen carriers.
Sun rays make no distinction.
Monsoon clouds rain without any confined jurisdiction.
Underground creatures share the earth
and live wherever desired without a fight.
Darkness prevails on half of earth at any one time
regardless of national boundaries at night
Trees don't ever go on strike.
Purify atmosphere for one all alike.
Breeze doesn't care about man-made dividing lines.
I don't know why then, man all over the world,
behaves worse than canines?
He's been foolish enough to divide land, sky, sea and
on top of all, hearts
No wonders, he stinks of incivility and rots.
Some propagate even division of outer space.
so that, he may morbid it's tranquility and sanctity
when, on earth he's even lost his trace.
His acts make this planet as a whole, stink
like a putrefied garbage bin.
Under some pretext or the other, strangely enough,
he justifies all his sin.

Canines may be very possessive of their territorial rights
but, are at least, loyal
Their master instead of learning from pets had opted
to be deceitfully selfish and towards
both inner conscience and others, most, callous & disloyal
Only a deadly attack by some organism from outside space
can make him feel the necessity of universal unity.
otherwise, his religion, national chauvinism, caste and creed
will keep him divided till eternity!
To my mind, he'll never mend his ways
until, through his nose, he pays!

* * *

WHAT'S THEIR FAULT?

Indian bride enters apprehensively her husband's
house with many a dream about her married life.
Soon, in some devil's home, her
dream get shattered and cut to pieces by brutal dowry knife.
Some don't ask but,
expect her or come over with money and gold
Some, at the time of marriage,.
shamelessly demand and get bold.
As long as her parents and brother's
for her peace sake, can meet
her in law's wishes, she is
shown affections and care.
Thereafter, they threaten her
with dire consequences
and say, 'we'll make an example out of her which would be
dreadful and rare'
To save own and that of
parent's honor, some commit suicide.
Some are drowned, beaten or
burnt to death in broad day light.
Unfortunately, bridegrooms due to malpractices inherent
in our system, keep the ends of justice at bay.
These devils in the garb of a husband
and their parents, fix yet
another marriage in some
other town, on another day.
For them, a sacred wedlock is
nothing but legalized way to
sex and squeeze for money.

What a pity, in our so called
civilized society, such demons
have all days bright and sunny.
By giving daughter, parents actually
have already given whatever they possess.
Maltreatment, beating, abuses,
threats to their daughter in
some other house cause them enormous
mental suffering, pain and duress.
Every parent must treat in their house
other's daughters as their own.
Real peace inside the
four walls of any house, lies in this fact alone.

* * *

THE DEATH GOD

There is no way I could
ward off Your call.
Like an expert cricket bat, wouldn't
miss a straight ball.
You have consumed countless
    so far.
Sympathy, compassion and pity with
you hold no bar.
Those, who have come, have to
    go one day.
Those who boast, have to bow
so do all say.
One has no option, but
most humbly respect your will.
One has to partake this cage.
leaving it absolutely cold and chill.
Actually, you help everyone by
inviting and thereby redeeming his
sufferings and privation.
Therefore, one should thankfully
and gladly go with you without
    any hesitation.
Therefore, one must practice
detachment from an early age.
So that, at the time of bidding
good bye, one is mentally
absolutely ready for that transformation stage.

You flit in life breath, so, you have
all the right to take it away,
Lucky are those, who, at that
moment, recite your name and
behold Your Divine aura and ray.

* * *

WATCH YOUR MOODS

Your mood,
has something to do with your food.
Weather has a lot of say.
and how's been the going over the day.
On the people you came across
and on the mood of your boss.
Thoughts that rake your idle mind.
upon interaction with people;
        both kind and unkind
On what your body is used to and
        what it got.
On your and your near and dear one's lot
Upon clothes that you wear.
kind of sufferings and privations over
the day that you had to bear
Remember, on your mood depends
that of many others who, are
directly involved with you in life
Therefore, you have to somehow
manage to have cheerful
disposition even when, you
brave tough times and strife.
With your deliberate efforts in
this regard, life would appear a cake-walk.
How much have you lived
through cheerful moods is, in
essence, your life's quality hall-mark.

* * *

WHAT A TREATMENT?

Somewhere I'm thrown to
vultures, crows for their grand feast
and somewhere, after a few days,
my head is truncated and preserved by relatives
and body given ceremonial burial at least.
Somewhere' I'm thrown into rivers from bridges
to be eaten by waiting vultures
and strange looking canines,
Somewhere I'm given ceremonial
send off, number of times.
Somewhere, I'm burnt in a great man made fire,
Somewhere, I'm sold out to a skeleton buyer.
Somewhere, I'm preserved with
my riches around.
somewhere, I'm buried alive
without anyone hearing a sound.
Somewhere, I'm shoed and dragged
Somewhere, before secret disposal
I'm gunny bagged.
When I'm warm, I perform for
others, such acts.
When I' m pale and cold, others do
the same to me as a matter of fact.
I'm of some use as long as
there exists in me, some fire.
When I'm cold, before long, I'm
kept on a pyre.

People want to meet me as long
as there is, in me, a glow
After all's over, the same people
perform such strange customs
without being slow.

* * *

HUMAN BODY

Like clear tea needs a strainer and
a horse owner needs a trainer.
Similarly, life needs a container
This container grows and then somewhat decreases in size,
many truths and lies remain hidden in its disguise.
Some containers are big and some, small.
Some short and some tall.
Some fair and some black,
some sealed and some, with a crack.
Some ugly and some attractive to look at.
Some with real good stuff inside and
some, only junk have.
Some by sheer chance and luck,
get placed in show windows under glittering lights.
Some remain hidden on a shelf out of everyone's sight.
Some are in a great demand and
on some, on lookers don't cast a glance.
All containers have their marking and wrappers
like, all babies look alike but,
are generally in different diapers.
All have pre written manufacturing and expiry date.
When will they reach consumer's house and
when will they be done with is a matter of sheer fate.
In these containers, life witnesses a constant struggle between
hope and despair.
People without any desire are indeed very rare.
Like customers are attracted by what's inside a container
and not, how outwardly it looks like,
similarly, in human containers
what's inside is worth a glance
and appreciation and not, what's outside.

* * *

TIMES DO COME WHEN CHIPS ARE DOWN

Time comes in everyone's life
when, one hears trumpet's sound on the other side loud & clear,
when, one experiences in dry
eyes, a silent tear.
When, dew drops on lush green
grass, sting like thorns.
one dreams only about being constantly
chased by Rhinos with their mighty horns.
When, star studded sky appears
like, about to rain down stones.
When, continuously chill and fear
enter deep into bones.
When, monsoon rain looks like
a rain of fire from hell.
when one constantly hears
the funeral bell.
When, it becomes more than
apparent that only marks and
scars of life are to go along.
I assume than, nothing
what-so-ever entertains one
not even, the most favorite song.
At such a time, only through
inner strength, one can triumph and rejoice,
provided, one feels the pulse of
inner rhythm and hear inner voice.

It's important to be self-sufficient
to face both life and death with smiles,
otherwise, this short span would look a
never ending forced march through
unknown miles.

* * *

MY VERY SPECIAL THANKS

Upon touching your feet, I
get electrified oh! my dear mother.
Comfort and pleasure that I
experience then, I, derive from none other,
Your love for me, is in its purest form
While carrying and rearing
me up, you must had
forborne happily many a storm!
What I am, is, what you've made.
For you, regardless of my deficiencies
and limitations, I'm more precious
than most expensive ornaments studded with jade.
I'm quite aware of your sacrifices.
Your affectionate cares and blessings keep me away
from all kinds of vices.
I feel helpless, when in times of
need, I can't even reach
like, that grain of sand which,
remains dry even though, it's part
of the sea beach.
Despite great distances, you
remain in my mind all the time.
Your benign cares, affections and
blessings spring in me many a thanks giving rhymes.
For you, I would always
remain a babe regardless of my age.
For me, you would always
be revered as a deity or a sage.

Your protective hands have
got me out of many an ordeal without a scratch.
Special significance to 'Mother's Thanks
Giving Day,' I attach.
I can't ever pay you back and be
quits for what you've done for me.
I'm lucky to have your,
continued benign blessings that be!

* * *

SELF APPRAISAL

I'm on my way out.
I sense fast approaching
end of this bout.
With every successive moment.
tea in my life's cup seems
to be getting cold.
Amply I realize now, that,
I'm getting old.
I think it's high time, I
take stock of things around now.
But, I'm so intricately webbed
that, I don't know which
end to start from & how!
Over the years, I got
unnecessarily busy with trifles
In fact, so busy I remained
that I didn't notice the
speed of passing currents & ripples.
I, myself created those, ripples
around me & disturbed my inner calm.
Never pondered about their
effect & impact & consequently
        caused spiritual harm.
surely at this stage, I can't
undo what I've done except,
        mend my ways.
Sweep that filth in me under
the brilliance of Divine rays.

At this rate, I'm bound to
get out of ring in a shameful manner.
After all, what standard of
leather can one expect from
      an amateur tanner?
I would soon fade out from
other's memory & get lost in
      oblivion of dead past.
I must know that I occupy
some slot in other's brain
only, as long as breath in
      me last.
I haven't lost everything as,
sometimes is still there.
All I need to do is, to
totally shake up my psyche &
for real better days, at least
      once dare.
Life in my present from is
      more than precious.
Without spiritual growth,
all other progress is just a farce
      & malicious.

* * *

HYPOCRISY

What's happened to human beings on earth?
Live throughout with hatred.
 greed and anger right from their birth!
Despite civilization, there is
no let up in human abuse.
People get on to other's throats on any excuse.
Some kill in the name of their prophet,
some for other's money and wallet.
Some for oil.
some for soil.
some for a quick buck,
some of neighbor's duck,
some for the sake of fun,
 exuberance and zest.
worst still is, that killers and terrorists
legitimize their dastardly acts
in the name of nationalism and patriotism.
Some attempt to veil these
under disguise of religious
 emancipation and chauvinism,
No one seems to think of
mother's, father's, son's, daughter's
brother's and sister's silent tears.
Instead, on mass killings, get
into pseudo national euphoric
moods and celebrate with cheers.

Until one-'n' all, regardless of
Caste, creed, religion and nationality,
treat others as their own.
people all over this world,
would continue to moan and groan.
How about bestowing upon
everyone here some real sense?
Otherwise, everyone on this
earth, would, live through
somehow, as absolutely insane & tense!

* * *

I'M ALSO A HUMAN BEING

I was born in tatters.
Since then, my body and soul have
been badly battered.
That's why to anyone, whether I live or
die, it doesn't matter.
No one loves me since, I'm born poor.
Whereas, everyone would have,
had I been rich, I' m sure!
I've lived all throughout with that
awful feeling, as if, I were a hunted fugitive.
Just because to anyone, I'd nothing to give
Abject poverty is the worst curse;
for a poor, in times of need,
there is no one to nurse.
My gnawing hunger and state
drives me to desperation.
I can do any crime on this world
for this wretched stomach, without any hesitation.
This hypocrite society, hates me
when, I perform acts of desperation
to fill my tummy.
For bringing me into this world
I keep cursing God, my dad and mummy.
I, too want to lead a life of respect and dignity.
There seems no hope to improve my life's quality.
Sheer helplessness and desperation,
made me do all heinous crimes.
Even, I forgot that self was a
human being at times.

Committing crime and sin, now, have
become my way of life.
Otherwise, how could I have survived?
Poor children anywhere in the
world, need, love and care.
Otherwise, for sheer survival,
any brutally savage and heinous
crime would they dare!

* * *

THE HIGH & LOW IN LIFE

Life went by unfolding some
good & some bad days.
Spells of bright sun & sometimes
    Without those benign rays.
Sometimes, I awoke into
fragrant, promising dawn's musk.
Sometimes, it ended up in
    a heart-jolting dusk.
Many a times, I pleaded
With Him saying why don't you punish
me once for all?
He won't listen & kept showing
    me His images both short & tall.
I'm grateful as, He kept tides
neither too high nor too low,
Probably. That's why, I could
keep a cool head even on
    shoe-bitten toes.
Blessed are those, who just
get one square meal over a day & yet
    sing & dance through
        their nights,
Breeze or no breeze, keep their
    kites on incredible heights.

Remember, when you tamper with life's
      natural flow,
it could deliver you a real
      hard blow.
Storms are there in everyone's
life both within & without
You've to brave these to ensure
that at the end of the road,
you aren't a big wash out!

* * *

WATCH YOUR SHADOWS

I notice, when, I get away from
source of light, only my false.
shadows keep growing in size.
That's why perhaps I shut my eyes
during the darkness of night & keep
    awaiting benign sun-rise.
When I'm exactly beneath that source,
    my pseudo shadows just
        disappear.
Nothing then, distracts my individuality
    or true self from far & near.
This source is light of wisdom that
      is inherent.
When it's right on top & takes over,
my whole body is synchronous &
      coherent.
When I sway away from that light
      of wisdom
I, only project false, pseudo & incorrect
    boundaries of my kingdom.
Materialistic delusions alone, pull
us into that area of darkness.
When we get disenchanted with
our false images, we get to that
source of light with unusual fastness.
To keep that light on & stay with
      it, is vital.
Otherwise, our stories would
remain without any worthwhile title.

* * *

LET PEOPLE SAY

Elephant walks by, most unconcerned,
when dogs bark.
Soldiers keep penetrating into
enemy lines even when it's pitch dark.
Sun doesn't get perturbed when
clouds stop its ray.
We. Too, shouldn't get unduly bothered
    about what people would say.
Since, most people around us,
have nothing much to do
    except, talk.
If they could help it, they would
ensure that you don't even
    step out for a walk.
However, in Indian society,
If you don't make an
unnecessary show of your wife,
riches and prayers,
it could save you from a lot of tears!
Everyone has the basic right to
live the way one likes to, of course,
    within civilized bounds.
Certainly our lives can't be
dictated and infringed upon by
    street dogs and hounds.

It never occurs to us that just because
there is a street dog outside we shouldn't
    go out of the house,
and not get friendly to someone, for the
    fear of getting in our hair, a louse
Remember, whatever is fated it
    Can't be wiped out.
Whatever, one is destined to get in life,
    one would get it,
        without a doubt.

* * *

EXPLORATION WITHIN

Within me, there is intensely deep and
dense darkness; more than jet black.
Perhaps, it's because wisdom of
    conscientiousness, that I lack.
How can I hope to sweep off
this darkness without
    a source of divine light?
Surely, at this rate, its intensity
would go on increasing, similar
    to phenomenon in moonless night.
Streak of hope is well in sight.
if, I could sieve from this world,
    what is absolute truth and right.
As of now, fear grips me, even
before, I venture out to explore this
    darkness inside.
Perhaps, because I know in it abundance of
only falsehood and lies lie.
Over my years, variety of venoms of
materialism have entered my body
That's why, life has turned out to
    be so shoddy
How can I blame anyone for
    this wretched and
    deplorable state?
All this time, my soul had been experiencing
a draconic and tormenting grate.

Mere realization at this stage,
    isn't enough.
I need to undergo penance
    and have my Golf ball
    somehow across the rough.
Surely, means and ends are
    in our own hand.
We can listen to desired radio
station, only when, we switch on the
    right frequency band!

* * *

A NATURE'S GIFT

You notice and get attracted
regardless, whether, I' m small or big.
like from top, you make out
on the sea below, an oil rig.
Most of you come close, smell me
and remark 'isn't that Cute'?
Some of you, in admiration, even
pluck me off my shoot.
You take me along for great
reunion and separation.
I'm invariably present for all
religious ceremonies and moments
    of jubilations.
Some of you, through me in silence, say out your heart.
To beautiful environments
around you, I, certainly play a
    great part.
To me, each one of you also,
appears to be a charming flower; everyone
with a distinct fragrance, size, colour and identity
budding, blooming and withering
    in my vicinity.
I get unhappy and unhealthy
    due to pollution of air and water that you
    cause in ignorance.
You don't realize that for
your own health and happiness too, it
    has a great significance.

Our collective existence depends
upon how much you care for
    ecological balance.
Believe you me, on it,
depends your world's biological
    balance!

* * *

AN ORPHAN'S SIGH

What was my fault for which,
soon after birth, I was left on a way side?
Just because, my unwed mother got
scared and wanted her immoral relationship to hide!
I wonder, if she had to abandon me
    helpless like this way,
Why did she carry me and nurture me
    inside day after day?
I'm now grown up somehow, but
    till date, I haven't met my mother.
My infancy, childhood and adulthood
    is gone by on mercies of other.
School children used to make fun of
me when, I couldn't tell them my father's name.
I used to feel as if, after committing
a dastardly sin, I was living without any shame.
There is someone somewhere,
who, undoubtedly must have had his fun.
But later, refused to accept me as his son.
Sometimes, I feel like searching him
and sorting him out with a gun.
My anger and rage knows no bounds.
If ever, I meet them, I would behave
    like hounds.
Why did they maltreat me in this wretched manner?
I carry in me now, an orphan's invisible mark and banner.
My life's been like, an unbaked cake.
What a price I had to pay for someone's
lack of courage, confidence and mistake!

* * *

YOUTH

Youth belongs to mind,
irrespective of number of years, left behind.
As long as, one keeps picking up world signals in positive
sense, one is young regardless of age.
Once, antennas are closed down, that's surely the end
    of life's page.
Youth is synonym of will
to wage struggle in life.
One is old regardless of one's
years, if and when, there are no
goals, pursuits and strife.
Heart and mind pump in vigor and vitality in body
without which, life's game
would look so shoddy!
It's a treat to see men and women
in their eighties displaying free fall
    from great heights.
Their skins may have had wrinkles but,
their spirits are like ever soaring up colorful kites.
When one's interest in life is over,
Old age regardless of years
then predominantly on One's head hover.
If you want to remain young till your death,
keep your interests alive and
pursue them vigorously till
    your last breath.
Remain involved with the world
    & be part of the herd!
Don't you ever cut yourself off &
close your hatchet,
other -wise, you'll surely kick the bucket!

* * *

HURRY BRINGS WORRY

If you cut out from life unnecessary hurry,
you would be able to ward off a lot of worry.
You get up late, laze around
and then in a bid to be in time, try and catch
    a running bus,
invariably get stuck in rush and slush.
Hurriedly go through the question
    in exam and start answering
    without due thought.
After writing many pages,
    generally realize your fault.
To be in time for a important
meeting, you speed up car,
generally buy trouble & while on road.

own and other' happiness you mar.
In a hurry, forget to carry office keys,
realize that you are without
abdomen guard only, when you
reach the popping crease.
Run across road without a careful glance.
Reach somehow, on the other
side by sheer luck and an odd chance.
This avoidable hurry cuts
    short your life span
Keep cool and live life of
discipline and temperance, if you can.

When, moments force tension on
you, it's time to stay cool.
Like still waters in a pool.
Remember, one who's always
in a hurry, is termed a big fool.

* * *

ONE DAY

It would be your last one,
Of course, you won't know that you're
    right there at the finish point
    of your life-run.
That day, you won't be able to wear
    your crown.
You would become a subject of past in
    your own town.
You would leave some tell-tale marks and
    some memories; both good and bad.
Some would describe you as gentleman
    and some as cad.
You would be lucky, if until then, all
    your body organs function normally.
Luckier still, if around you, some gather
    and give you a send off formally.
Some get to know what is to follow.
Some, by then, with concerted and constant
efforts upgrade their souls and some remain
    spiritually bankrupt and hollow.
For some, last moments are that of agony and pain.
Some call it a day as absolutely insane
Yet, for a few, those moments are full of joy
    and ecstasy;
very peaceful and ushering them into divine
    fantasy.
Remember, that fateful day would dawn
    earlier than you anticipate.
Therefore, how about upgrading yourself to
the extent that, instead of crying then, you
    could celebrate!

* * *

GRAND FINALE

I'm now old.
Surely, my body would soon get cold.
Life seems to be getting out of my hold.
I'd covered great distances, met many and
left a few casts out of this mould.
To face it's end, I must prepare self to be cheerful and bold.
Sitting in my easy chair, my eyes gaze and
stare into my past as far back as I remember.
I get an overall impression that I
enjoyed this club as a respectable member.
Now, I realize, since, the going was good,
how fast I'd gone through this otherwise, a great mess!
just like, unpredictable time span of a game of chess.
In my last phase only, I reckoned no one
in this materialistic world, had
        time for poor and old.
True images of everyone around, become
more clear as time unfold.
Expectations of paying attention to you
from anyone as you did for other in your
hay-days is more than just.
Solace lies in finding and having His
company in the final phase with
        unflinching faith and trust.
Therefore, when this world forgets you,
diversion of your mind towards Him is a must.
Otherwise, despite mortal blows and shocks,
you'd remain till your very last, engulfed with
        materialistic love and lust.

Experience of others show that everyone's
inner sense prompts him saying balloon is now about to burst.
Some then, get unusually sober and some, super-active.
Some exhibit patience and some, become hyper-reactive.
I don't know whether my grand-finale
is going to be cheerful or sad.
That's certainly the ring test of how
much up-liftment or degradation my soul
    in this cage had!

* * *

AFTER YOU'VE GONE

World would go on the same way.
Just that you won't be there for any more day.
Fact of life is that, no one is indispensable.
In-fact, you are similar to a commodity
        which is expandable.
In your own house, at best to begin with, there
would be a framed and garlanded photograph.
Soon, it would pick up dust, fungus and daft.
It would then be moved out of its original
place to some neglected dark and dingy corner.
Garland tattered, frame ant-eaten, glass
cracked, snap not worth a mourner.
Some, would remember you on the day
you vanished from where you came.
Remember, your great grandsons and perhaps,
grand children won't even know your name.
You're only instrumental in introducing
new actors to this world stage.
They'll have to perform according to
the pre written script page by page.
Therefore, don't have illusion that without
        you, other's life, would stand still.
Hence, don't unnecessarily kill yourself
Every day while going through life's rut and mill.
Try and make your soul's future bright,
by being honest, truthful, loyal and acting
        always right.
Sooner you realize, better it would be.
otherwise, this materialistic life is
a fool's paradise for Thee.

* * *

WHO IS MORE CIVILISED?

Animals don't ever over eat.
Go on voluntary fast to
regain internal body rhythm and heat.
Chimps and Gorilla generally don't fight,
only by their chest beating and
growls cause scare & fright.
Peacocks, pigeons, doves dance around
    and try to woe their partners heart.
Fowls, Monkeys, dogs and many others
before claiming, their mate, have to exhibit and prove,
physical prowess's on their part.
Ants follow footsteps and work like hell,
honey bees go miles away collecting
nectar but always return to
that bee-hive only where they dwell.
Carnivores generally remain
hungry during antelope's mating and
    breeding time.
Generally, they respect other's territorial
sovereignty and don't indulge in
    cunning, & heinous crimes.
They don't stalk young ones
    instead, those who've seen life.
Most birds after mating, help each
other, in making their nest and together
    put up their strife.
He Beaver makes a beautiful nest
    before seeking she Beaver's hands.
Grazing animals, while looking after each other's
young ones, move together into distant lands.

Most of them, regardless of species,
raise alarm whenever, there's
      some danger to life in general
Crows, monkeys, elephants etc express
grief and shock on fellow being's death and
appear, to accord; a community funeral.
Generally, all respect their fair sex,
remain loyal and show love and affections.
Live together sharing
nature's bounty, without causing afflictions.
Certainly, today's man, is worse than
      birds, insects and animals.
This, so called most civilized species of
all, is actually worse than aboriginal cannibals.

* * *

WHAT A DIFFERENCE!

When your butterfly's gone,
everything is there except heart is without beat.
All's intact except, body is without heat.
Eyes no longer react to any light.
Body rests flat on four shoulders without any height
Nostrils no longer blow.
Face is without any glow.
Skin is sensitive to neither cold nor hot.
Mind, for a change, is without any thought.
Despite riches and fortunes,
palms are absolutely empty and bare.
    Body no longer needs anyone's care..
Lines on right palm, instead of future, point towards past.
There's no cosmic energy whatsoever, left in the cast.
Cats, Dogs and other Carnivores
in near vicinity, don't get a scare
Any kind of threatening and dangerous
environment no longer raise a hair.
All rights stand forfeited except, the last right.
Time is turned into just an eternal dark night.
In nut shell, this world is, as long as
your butterfly is there.
Otherwise, the perishable and mortal is left behind here.
Remember, your near & dear ones in a great
hurry, as per religious rituals would remove you for good
form the scene.
With you having gone forever, after a thorough wash your
house is made to look once again neat & clean.
Soon, being out of sight, you would be out of everyone's mind.
Your acts would flash across to a few if only,
those were selfless, benevolent and kind.

* * *

PRAGMATISM

LIVE EVERYDAY

Life isn't a bed of roses,
Occasionally, you keep getting happy and unhappy doses.
When times are bad, you plunge into
        unfathomable depths of despair,
start saying every moment 'I don't care.'
On every happening, you seek in utter disgust, explanations.
What others are doing then, are your only attractions.
On every conceivable misfortune, you start saying why me?
Egoism fattens your head and you feel that for all locks,
        only you, possess the key.
You get more bothered about what others will say,
        keep thinking only of your past day.
All this is bound to take you nowhere
except, amidst ever increasing frustration, disgust and despair.
Thus, you invite yourself unnecessary and uncalled for strife.
All this effects your love, children and family life.
You can usher in a dramatic change without a sweat.
Honestly, it is without any fume and fret.
When confronted with an awkward one,
be brave & have a smile.
Be calm even if, he stirs up his bile.
Don't you ever jump to conclusions
        as you'll often frighten the best ones away.
Even amidst the worst,
        count His blessings and learn to be careful & gay.
If you visit a surgical ward, orphanage and cremation grounds
        once a day, you'll never go wrong.

These would have such a sublime effect
      that you be really happy life long.
Simplicity, honesty, and truthfulness
      will make you a darling of all.
Remember, life is a soccer game in which, you have to somehow,
make sure that you alone keep kicking the ball.

* * *

WAY TO PEACEFUL LIFE

Rarely have I come across a happy and contented man in life.
Despite materialistic pleasures, rich accumulated religious
experience of forefathers, his life is full of mental agony and
strife.
What's that bothers man today, and causes
within him vibrations other than those of peace and bliss?
It's undoubtedly a subject of genuine concern of
all mankind worth a kiss.
Today, man really can't be blamed for his values and their
emptiness.
Since his childhood, he's been taught to appreciate things
unrelated to truth and real happiness.
It's high time to realize that we have become
victims of our own values and state of mind.
That's why, we leave the pristine divine happiness,
that all of us experience in our childhood, far behind.
We don't realize that how we live is important
and not how long is this life.
we get engrossed with only materialistic strife.
We busy ourselves with temples, mosques and
religious ceremonies to heap His love without loving His
creation.
We busy ourselves with numerous pleasure hunts and drives
not knowing that they are poor substitutes for happiness and
lead us to frustration.
We busy ourselves in getting entangled in the silky webs
of cosmic delusions turning deaf ears
to inner promptings.
Yet, at the end, all of us expect from this
meaningless life a purposeful ending!

We busy ourselves in working for own glamour
and glory totally forgetting that of God.
We busy ourselves in attaining greater materialistic heights
without conquering 'self Lord.'
As a result, man leaves this world. crying the way he came
Then, his soul wanders pitifully in His 841akh forms of
creation frame.
God has given us sight to see His greatness and
mind to understand Him.
Sight helps in realizing His existence and mind in finding Him.
The cosmic delusions only attack the mind and
impair its comprehension and judgments.
Anger, greed, pride and attachment are thus
the natural increments.
Our pride, pseudo-egoism and expectations go beyond our logic.
They torment and stifle our heart, minds and turn the story
tragic.
Haven't we suffered enough by going along
the ways of the so called civilized world?
It's high time we retire to the world within us,
which, speaks a language altogether different.
As years go by, everyone seems to be growing only in age,
his selfishness and pride get him pity and unusual rage.
He doesn't listen to the promptings of the genuine
friend within his body cage.
At the fag-end, deceits self by behaving like pseudo sage,
By identifying with the Ocean, a drop of water becomes
part of it,
otherwise, it would stand isolated and without any stature.
We'll begin to experience many wonderful moments of fantasy
and blissful joy once we've identified with nature.
When the going is bad, even own shadows disappear.
When it's good, unheard people as near and dear from
nowhere, appear.
All materialistic relations are false.

It's a reality rather harsh.
Undoubtedly, the ways to wealth are many but to
universal truth only one which, lies beyond our selfish pursuit.
Truth is reality, reality God, God purity and
from purity comes feelings without which, man is a big fool.
It is hope which lies at the heart of all creations,
and it's this hope, which is, source of all distress,
despair and frustration.
Expectations in life bring invariably misery and gloom.
Shed it off and expect nothing from any one, not
even from your own body &live with the strength of soul
and then experience the same life without a groan.
If you can slash hope and desire,
there is no difference between you and your creator.
There is a unique pleasure in sharing our joys with other.
It is only then, life appears meaningful and
brings in its fold a purposeful death.
Otherwise, it is just another heap of breath over breath.
Let inner vibrations take over your head and heart and
goad you to do good.
Your actions will let you experience unfathomable
pleasures as much as you could.
Count His blessings by visiting orphanage and
hospital once a day,
feel the change in you and see your life turning gay.
For peace and stability, nothing like temperance;
It's a magic key to life full of roses and fragrance.
Unless one is tuned with inner-self and live
a peaceful life within,
It's a sheer waste and whole life stinks like a garbage bin.
Unless one is in complete control of self with
unflinching faith and firm resolve,
life will remain mysteriously dark and this riddle,
man, unable to solve.

* * *

LAUGHTER; THE BEST MEDICINE

What good is your life
If, you didn't laugh a while?
Laughter is the panacea of all ills.
Body gets motivated to leave all kinds of chills.
Laughter begets laughter,
with it, this otherwise tardy life, gets softer.
He is admirable who, could laugh in duress.
It's an application of vanishing cream on skin
under the influence of weather stress.
One who laughs, has company,
his heart and mind are in good symphony.
Laughter dispels fears of unknown.
Man with good sense of humor is never alone.
Humor cultivates wit and wit, humor.
Both don't let one fall a prey to any rumor.
Laughing at others is being foolish.
Laughing at someone when he is in trouble,
is being mulish.
Laugh at the appropriate time and place is being wise.
Blood gushes and sunken spirits then rise.
Laughter in life means health,
which is, the most precious wealth.
One who laughs and makes others laugh is the most sought by all.
Humorous man will have the whole town with his pall.
Witty sense of humor add to one's charm.
Remember, Charlie Chaplin humored the world by storm.
Humorous men live long,
their memories are always fresh and strong.
Charlie is today known to more than Churchill.

All sorts of germs plaguing the peace of our world,
for sure, this pill of laughter could kill.
It's recognized and appreciated by all, regardless of caste and creed.
It's undoubtedly the best medicine indeed.
It's spice to life,
like nectar in a hive
Life is as it is, tiresome &
therefore, let us sing and laugh it away.
This attitude will turn every moment in your life happy & pretty gay.

* * *

STRESS AND STRAIN

All kinds of stress and strain
sprout and are experienced somewhere in the brain.
It's both physical and mental.
The one out of love episode,
although very painful, yet, is sweet and gentle.
Our, this God- given body is great;
More you comfort it, more it yearns,
more you grill it, harder it turns.
Even, too much of happiness causes a peculiar fatigue.
A lazy man experiences too much of it
as both his body and mind are in league.
Attachment is the biggest source of pain,
materialistic illusions and delusions are the biggest bane.
Virtually they make a man unstable and insane.
Each worldly loss is like a blow on knuckles of hand
from a teacher's cane.
Sufferings and mental afflictions are rather acute
on those who live a pseudo life and feign.
Can anyone in open, hope to be dry
under a spell of torrential rain?
People try detachment too late in life
and hence, all efforts go in vain.
Outward involvement and inward detachment,
is a well recognized viable and practicable way.
One could attend to social duties and obligations
and yet, remain always blissfully gay.
Inner happiness, satisfaction and contentment
are more valuable.
You could thus make materialistic stress and strain
easily bearable.

* * *

MY SACRED MISSION

Here is yet another road that I'll tread or bike.
With a hope to find someone of my type & like
Hand in hand, we'll sing for love and peace,
in the service of poor and needy, keep our lives on lease.
I'm sure, I'm going to meet many
who would love to come with me,
and throw off robes of pseudo-egoism and hypocrisy
and become both in heart and mind what,
He has asked us to be.
There is no true peace even if, one
in billions, is without.
There is no cause for rejoicing anywhere,
if one amongst us, is without a house.
The truth and purity in me, goads me to go ahead.
In its pursuit, fears and horrors of unknown,
I must shed.
Peaceful men all over the world, for the peace of this world,
have to somehow find ways and means to unite.
In fight against poverty, illiteracy, hunger and chauvinism,
must they contribute all their mite.
In peace, man by the turn of the century, can turn out to be
super human.
Without it, his empire will be dead and forgotten as that of the Roman.
Don't you think the mission of Universal peace and
brotherhood is noble and sacred?
Come'n' join me regardless of my caste, creed and nationality
without any hatred.

* * *

JESUS IN FLESH AND BONE

At 'Mridul Hriday' (Tender Heart), I saw angels at
work for destitute.
Selfless devotion, sincerity and extreme
compassion fragranced their life attitude.
They're living symbols of human kindness and virtue,
In their thoughts, how best can solace and
peace be given to afflicted souls, is the only issue.
Their source of inspiration is Jesus himself;
in the garb of Mother Teresa.
Whose virtuous, devout Christian life,
makes her far prettier than legendary Mona Lisa.
She's a halo around of 'Service before Self',
compassion and divine humility,
materialistic illusions and delusions
of the world for her are nonentity.
A leper, destitute and homeless old in Calcutta slums,
looks upon her as Jesus incarnate.
While dying in her lap, showers blessings, and is
wonder struck-with her divine trait.
She cleans their defecation, bathes them and feed,
irrespective of their caste, color and creed.
She distributes immense love to those who, are
remorseful of their bad deed.
She doesn't give sermons on Bible but, believes in actions.
Her whole celibate and virtuous life, has unique attractions.
'Love His creation' is her only message.
Because, sincerity, dedication, humility only, help make it a
trouble-free passage.

* * *

MENTAL BLOCK

Body is your temple and
God somewhere within,
whereas, in the name of God and religion
you perpetuate only sin.
Don't think when you kill others in the
name of Allah or Ishwar, you'll be
destined to heaven.
You' re bound to get hell as deserves any demon.
It beats my imagination, how you get convinced
that your God will be pleased if, you kill others.
You'll surely get His wrath for orphaning innocent children and
widowing mothers.
All religions preach love of mankind,
whereas you, in the name of religion, become a
savage beast devoid of civilized mind.
If, you keep your religion confined within you
and be with Him at all times,
you will be revered like a monumental sacred shrine.
You've no right to take other's life on any pretext.
Don't bring in religion and stir up emotions under,
yours and other's chest.
Loving Him and His creation is the only sacred duty.
It is selfless love which can make you understand
the real definition of beauty.
You all acknowledge that Ishwar, Allah, Christ and Guru Nanak
are all manifestations of one God.
Since, all have preached universal love and brotherhood,
rule of love and not by iron rod.
Interpretations of our religions are more than absurd
and suit our convenience.

We sacrilege our respective faiths and take undue advantage
of our God's lenience.
We have no right to preach what we don't understand.
Major issues we merrily forget, but on unimportant ones,
for vested gains, must we take war-like stand!
By following any religion in true letter and spirit,
one can only do good to humanity,
regardless of caste and creed.
Remember, He will punish you beyond tolerance
for your each wrong deed.

* * *

TRUTHFUL RIPPLES

How lonely I'm amongst billions around?
It's an absolute truth, though, absurd it may sound.
My superficial relations are based on the principle of
'give and take.'
Pseudo-cosmic delusions put the credibility of my
conscience at stake.
Life goes on as no one is indispensable.
Best time of my life, of course, I was unaware then, was,
when I kicked around in the cradle.
I've yet to realize His company although He is within me.
I've yet to thank Him for his countless blessings, that be.
Clock ticks away time which, for anyone,
is predestined and unalterable.
I must show superficial involvement with
worldly chores and squabble.
For stability and peace of mind, there is no need to wander
and unnecessarily sweat.
I've to bridle my demands
and think of repaying His debt.
Otherwise, what good are my eyes?
the value of which, only blind can recognize!
What good are my ears?
Whereas ton load of silence constantly a deaf bears!
What good are my fingers and nails,
worth of which, only lepers appreciate.
What good are my riches,
if the very sight of a poor, I continue to hate!

Everyone keeps cribbing about shoes
till one comes across a lame.
You've got to be grateful to Him as He gave you
this beautiful form and parents who gave you a name
When will You help me remove my ignorance?
When will I help You spread Your universal message and benevolence?

* * *

TRY IT

Little acts of goodness and appropriate smiles
will endow you with that divine radiance
and keep all evils away miles.
Life gets punctuated with meaningless routine.
Time flies away like a dream.
We don't care if our actions, san humaneness,
politeness and humility.
Thus, we, day in and out, perpetuate the spirit of deviltry.
Divine wisdom rests in us so, let us not subdue.
For all your mental afflictions, requisite patience
has the clue.
Time gone by is your past.
There's no good realizing its value when one nears one's last.
Remind yourself time and again, what you came for
and what are you doing.
Otherwise, there is no end to your wailing and wooing.
Human form is the most precious dress of your soul.
To serve the suffering humanity, your steps must be
extraordinarily courageous and bold.
True test of your character is what you do
when, you know, others won't know.
remember, you will reap only what you sow!

* * *

WHY DO YOU?

Why do you worry about your future when you
know it's going to remain unaltered?
Why do you fret and fume over materialistic happenings,
when you know they remain unchartered?
Why do you lay so much stress on
your tomorrow and kill your today?
Why do you keep your internal eyes shut and at the end,
hope to see that divine ray?
Why don't you fathom your part in His drama?
Why don't you ponder and-act righteously
in the pursuit of lord Krishna's divine gospel of 'karma[15]'
Why don't you stir out of your materialistic trance
and achieve real peace?
Why don't you maintain peace in your internal
rhythm by just going on the path of honesty at least?
Why do you live through self created moments
of hopes and despair?
Why do you always think of only your own comfort and care?
Why do you prefer to shut your eyes
when you see someone in trouble?
Why don't you understand how uncertain and transitory
is the life of an air bubble?
Why don't you realize His greatness
in whatever, you look at?
Why do you close your eyes in broad day-light, like a bat?
Every moment is precious than Gold.
Take that first step in right
direction and be bold.
Why do you get emotional and lose your
sense of balance?

Why do you get petered out when you are
required to accept a sinner's challenge?
Why don't you attempt to achieve
spiritual enhancement?
Why don't you understand the real meaning of word;
advancement?
Why do you blame others for your bad days?
Why do you shun His company
when, He, within you stays?
Why do you get happy and dismayed over what people say?
Why do you get stifled when you have to brave a hot
and uncomfortable day?
Why don't you practice divine temperance
and experience real peace?
Why don't you help the needy and taste
that divine feast?
Always remember Him to be very kind and benevolent.
If you have faith, He will get you out of any mess,
without a dent.
Your only one sincere attempt,
will make you look through right and wrong
Don't let this precious life, in
human form, go waste for a song!

* * *

LIVE TO LOVE

Live to love.
rather than love to live.
Shun thoughts of getting something from someone,
instead, harbor thoughts to give.
Live and let live,
and, experience that bliss when, you unselfishly give.
Life is worth living.
This world is worth giving.
Live to give
even, your own life.
Loving poor, destitute and hapless
is worth a blissful strife.
Selfish love and living for self alone,
undoubtedly, makes anyone experience
a galore of moan and groan.
Alas! everyone seems to live for self and none for others.
Why can't we all learn this blissful lesson from our mothers?
Her love is selfless and pure.
Her blessings; a blissful cure.
Other's life deserves love and respect.
Love alone can make your existence justified and perfect.
His entire creation is worth loving since He loves all.
Giving finishing touches to His glorious drama
is worth an effort rather than, we let it stall.
So, live to love without greed.
Love immensely without bothering caste and creed.
Your genuine love will generate a chain reaction.

Tremendous energies thus released
will provide all a blissful protection.
It's the only way to kill
all kinds of germs of social,
political and religious infection.
Try it and reinforce His glory.
You could surely provide that required healing
touch to this otherwise, awfully tragic story.

* * *

A CURSE ON HUMANITY

During one of my train journeys, on a busy platform,
I felt hungry.
I's attracted by a stall, which had many a eatable
and pastry.
The stall-owner saw my pockets promising,
& quickly offered me piping hot food that I indicated.
I couldn't resist the temptation of devouring it
even without being properly seated.
I's so hungry that, I finished more than half,
unmindful of my immediate surroundings.
My concentration on eating was so acute that I
didn't bother to cast a glance even at my belongings.
All of a sudden, I experienced a strange feeling;
some body's gaze was fixed on me which, sent my mind reeling.
Willy- nilly, I look one more helping and looked into
the staring eyes which, had disturbed
my concentration.
I realized that it was, the un-flickering gaze of a boy;
crippled with mal-nutrition.
By the side of him, there rested a skinny dog who,
also, gazed at me with his tongue lolling out.
They're all set to grab the remnants that I
may throw after a fight out.
Lad's head, unusually big, stomach bulging out under
his pigeon's chest invited both
sympathy and hate.
His bones weak, deformed and legs ever refusing to
withstand his skeleton's weight.
He was replica of crude curse of hunger and starvation,

I wondered, if there would be any count of his sufferings
and privation!
In his big and black eyes, there were tears,
the dog would claim the remnants and he would go
without a piece were, his obvious fears.
The whole sight was so cruel and pathetic
that I felt no more desire for any food.
Depressed, I plunged into a sad and pensive mood.
I ordered food for both and took it to be a rare chance.
Boy bestowed on me a thanks giving glance.
When he held food in his hands, tears of joy
and happiness welled up in his eyes.
The fact that, I could help out a needy, soared
my spirits to heavenly skies.
I felt pleased with self recapturing his parting glance
of gratefulness and gratitude.
It's then, I realized the sufferings manifested in
poverty and its magnitude.
If, people all over the world, have two square meals a day
instead of three,
Our planet will be malnutrition, hunger and starvation free.
When you see someone without a smile and give him
one of yours,
the joy and bliss that you experience, is undoubtedly,
bone thrilling and pure.
If all 'Haves' consider ensuring square meals to
'Have Nots' as their moral and public duty,
I'm certain, that our world society, on its own
will get rid of all crime and cruelty.

* * *

THAT'S THE WAY IT IS

Moon increases & decreases in size, as if, lives & dies.
Ascent & descent are inherent in life, as if,
two faces of the same coin.
Like, so distinct & different in looks are head & tail of a lion.
All kingdoms in past, reached the climaxes
of their power & then, got completely wiped out.
Gain & loss are enshrined in every facet of life, no doubt.
Everyone grows to zenith of physical beauty & power
but, soon degradation & degeneration of cells
commences heralding the final hour.
Therefore, there's no wisdom in vanity,
as, affording everyone,
various climaxes is just His Divine amenity.
It's good to think big
but better, to stay at mother earth.
One can be peaceful if one secures & ensures
safety of one's hearth.
Similarly, before buying a piece of land, for settling down,
One has to analyze it's pros & cons & ups & downs
Remember, even the most sober & gullible
variety of Canine, when driven against wall,
can turn into a ferocious hound.
Life, in to doubt complex, yet not all that hard to understand.
Those, who think & act rationally & dispassionately,
can only, turn their stories unusually grand!

* * *

BITTER TRUTH

With dead roots, a tree can't survive,
Without breath, there can't be life.
With grey hair, one can't look young,
there can't be peace, without
the use of benign and soft tongue.
With incompatible company, one
    continues to live aloof,
without support pillars, there can't be a roof.
With hearsay in a court of law, you can't prove
Without effort, nothing would move.
With betrayals, life can't be peaceful,
Without truthfulness and sincerity, nothing
    could be meaningful.
With weak and timid mind, body
    can't have real power,
without God, thorns of life can't be
    crowned with flower.
With lies & deceit in heart,
one can't have friends.
without faith in Him, one would
    lose balance over life's bends.
With a plain glass, one can't see own images,
without His blessings, one can't
perceive truth behind cosmic mirages.

* * *

EXPERIENCE THE IMPOSSIBLE

One can experience rain even
    when sky is absolutely clear.
Taste Gin and Lime while holding
    a glass of Beer.
Walk through dense forest lane
in pitch dark night without any fear,
experience joy, even while,
there rolls down the cheeks, a tear.
Feel great distance from someone even
    when he is physically very near.
Run Marathon with calf muscle sheered.
Live with the vigor and vitality of youth
even when, one has white beard.
Walk straight despite a hunch-back.
Smile through ups and down of life without a brash.
Dash across bad stretches
    without a second thought.
feel comfortable and at peace
even when, it's miserably hot.
Seek happiness and contentment
    out of whatever is one's lot.
Find the vastness even in a dot.
All of it and much more, is
possible if, one possesses a positive mind,
and a heart; simple, straightforward and kind.

* * *

A LINK BETWEEN PAST AND FUTURE

Like sea is sometimes calm and
sometimes rough,
so is life, which is, one day
smooth and another day, rather tough.
What's going to happen is
always a great mystery.
At the end of it, people term it
a part of history.
Rather than one's past or future,
present is most important.
Only lessons of the past are however,
sacrosanct.
Present makes one's past and
future good or bad.
Present would determine whether
one would turn out to be a gentleman or cad!
Present is nothing but, what you
think and act.
Cumulative effect of your
actions, which is your present, makes past
and future as a matter of fact.
Thinking about future without
putting in earnest effort, is inviting
frustration and despair.
Whereas, being sincere in thought and action is rather fair.
Generally, success kisses feet of those, who dare.
Therefore, management of anyone's present,
needs utmost care.
Life goes on from one moment to
another, which is present.

Therefore, each moment if gainfully
spent, can make entire span
rather pleasant.
What was one's present once upon
a time, is now one's past.
Remember, future is, what
one's present would cast.
Past generally invites tears whereas, future only our fears.
Only present, if carefully managed, could
bring about smiles & cheers.
Obviously, our future depends on our own choice.
therefore, let us handle our present (Gods own
present to all of us) and rejoice!

* * *

CHALLENGE OF LIFE

Birth and death are a mere universal routine,
like smoking is accompanied with effects of killer;
Nikotine.
One follows the other without a miss.
The gap in between
the two realities is however, worth a kiss.
Facing challenges of life as
they pose, is living a life of purpose and meaning.
Being shy of them, is a negative mental attitude and leaning.
Since, someone else has given
life, therefore, it is He alone,
who has the right to take it away.
It is actually, cowardice on
the part of any one, who
prematurely attempts to call it a day.
Life for none here, is a
bed of roses,
it's a judicious mix of sweet,
sour and bitter medicine dozes.
Those, who don't doze up,
remain confined to a bed,
and are as good as a living dead.
Everyone passes through this
way just once.
Yet, people after thousands
of years, distinguish between
an angel and a demon for instance.
Life story is accumulation
of actions performed during
each and every breath.

Since, its primarily each breath alone,
that denotes life and death.
living for others selflessly,
is a real challenge.
Those, who accept it, can only achieve
meaningful spiritual growth and excellence.
Actually, one has to be a good friend to all
and rest automatically follows.
That's is the surest way to ensure
that life doesn't remain meaningless and hollow.

* * *

A SUBJECT MOST MISUNDERSTOOD

East and West are two great supplements.
Achievements of both to collective
humanity are great compliments:
One stands for spiritual growth
And the other, for materialism.
Undoubtedly, a judicious mix of both
Can give rise to balanced humanism.
Like a pauper can't help another pauper,
A bottle can't hold anything in
it without a proper stopper.
A rich man alone can help those,
Who need his help,
spiritual strength alone, would
Help him utilize for a good cause his wealth.
Being rich and being in a position
to help the needy is materialism.
Inner urge to help the 'Have Not's &
suffering humanity is spiritualism.
Therefore, both are a must.
Balanced rhythm and genuine quest for both
is rather just.
Those, who profess that materialism
and spiritualism are poles apart,
obviously don't understand the
inter-se relation of a horse and cart.
I feel both East and West have to from
each other, learn a lot.
In order to establish a very healthy
and cordial relationship
between the 'Haves' and Have Not's.

Take the example of Japanese,
who denote today, a perfect
synthesis of East and West,
most of them, that's why, possess
worldly riches along with inner peace and rest.
Why can't we. all practice the same?
Learn from each other without
any complex or shame!

* * *

WISDOM

God has made no one perfect;
    Not even, the majestic peacock
who, Looking at his legs & feet, gets a rude shock.
Had He done that, who could call this majestic bird
    imperfect?
The realization itself, makes one
remember Him with reverence as a matter of fact.
it's for us to realize our short comings
& then make genuine efforts to overcome.
That's how near perfection is achieved by some.
The sting in one's tongue & tail
Can bring about in one's life an
unforgettable storm & gale.
Vanity due to looks, physique, status, riches & wealth,
adversely effects psyche, life's freedom & general health.
Habit of telling lies,
makes one invariably cry & heave sighs.
A hypocrite, snooty & a show off is made out
& despised by all.
complexes steal away one's strengths &
don't let one grow in real terms strong & tall.
Innate goodness lies in correct self assessment & evaluation.
Coupled with sincere & genuine efforts of corrections
without any inhibition & hesitation.

* * *

EAT TO LIVE

Most people live only to eat.
Every day, own records of previous consumption they beat.
Net result is, that, they get heavier & heavier each day on their feet.
Their accumulated fat & obesity compels them to keep
    sticking to their seat.
Then, in order to continue to eat,
They run towards health clubs & go on crash diet course.
But, soon enough, they get back to square one as,
they don't remove the basic cause or source.
They soon realize the kind of harm they've caused to their body
& then, eat only easily digestible substitutes or
fat-free foods which were earlier considered more than shoddy.
Thus, they reduce their life-span.
Also, no worthwhile woman looks at them as a man.
Whereas, some people eat only to subsist
& generally hold a healthy and active life in their own fist.
There's no dearth of food on our planet if, all of us become;
people of above said second category!
It would help usher in a new chapter in man-kind's history.
Then, no one anywhere, would die of starvation,
Nowhere children would show signs of malnutrition.
Our world society would, at least, get rid of hunger-related, crimes,
All of us thus, would kill two birds with one stone and help
create better times.

* * *

YOU OUGHT TO BEHAVE

River waters race down to be where a great mass of water lies.
Without love in this world, life rushes into untold miseries & sighs.
Man's history is full of wars, hatred and greed.
Despite the fact that, since times immemorial, he'd been
calling himself a peace loving breed,
Why doesn't this so called civilized world, hear widow's and
    orphan's crying and wailing?
Their fate is like that of a letter on which address
is not penned down before mailing.
Everyone seems to profess and sound big.
Most people forget that they too, can fall into pits
    that for others, they dig.
People conveniently forget that example is
    better than prefect,
& the fact that no one is born perfect.
Life no doubt, despite man-made privations, somehow goes on
But imagine the advent of that dawn, when life anywhere on
planet would be without selfishness, hatred and greed!
All living and singing together without a thought of caste & creed.
That kind of qualitative change is the need of the hour.
Otherwise, for all mankind, grapes would ever remain sour.

* * *

FEARS AND WORRIES NEVER HELP

Everyone has fear of unknown.
People express it through their face, expression and tone.
Unnecessarily, We keep thinking what lies ahead.
Self created fears, worries, anxieties, and concerns keep one
engrossed during day and even on night bed."
A heavy dose of it, makes one feel, as if, a living dead.
"Do your duty and leave everything to me"
Perhaps, that's why Hindu's god; lord Krishna, had said.
Since, results depend on many an intangible factor,
We have to believe that our lives,
right from inception in womb, remain protected by that invisible protector.
Everyone depends on him so helplessly; even,
for each breath.
If He wishes, one would get out of a situation in which,
    there's sure death.
Young Indian bride's fears, before her
departure to her unknown husband's house, are understandable.
So is true of fighter pilots, in times of war, before a scramble.
But, big question is,
how do such worries and anxieties help?
Except, one has to get ready to face forthcoming situations
    after tightening one's belt.
Life without worries,
fears and anxieties would be so beautiful!
Solace lies in forgetting results and in just
being conscientiously dutiful.

* * *

HOW LONG WILL WE SUFFER?

Somewhere, a storm is beginning
to settle and somewhere, about to rise.
Net result is, mammoth human
misery and sufferings in their disguise.
Man-made storms are worst than
    the natural ones,
In them, there is more savagery
and brutality due to enormous power of
    both money and guns.
All over the world, killings
murders, kidnappings of innocent
is the order of the day.
Innate goodness of mankind is
either in hibernation or is being
compelled to be kept at bay
Whereas, in stirring up that bright
spark that, dwells in all, alone,
answer to these devastating storms lay.
Non-interference in other's affairs,
non-violence mutual respect
are the only, cardinal principles on which,
this world could possibly survive
Otherwise, stone-age days, all
of us, are destined to revive

* * *

GUESS WHAT?

I've known a lady, who one fine
morning out of the blue,
pronounced a candid clue.
"My time is up, put me on ground &
ensure till my last, I keep
hearing 'Gita'[16] recitation sound.
Within ten minutes, she called it
a day in a very peaceful way
Thanking one 'n'-all and the
bright sun of that day.
I've met a boy of eight
years, who told his father that
he would like to change his home and clan.
Father laughed it out saying,
"Well son, I have no such plan."
Sure enough, Within that week, one night the boy slept
never to see the dawn of next morning.
Father was perplexed and aghast on
his son's prophetic warning.
My healthy father wrote down in his private diary
just two days prior to his departure, his desire,
Obviously he'd read writing on wall
and announced quietly that he was soon destined to fire.
Some lucky ones, get to know what's in store.
There are innumerable such
examples in our rich folk-lore.

Why don't we always keep
this eternal truth in mind,
while we're up and about?
That's the only way we could,
emerge victorious at the end of
that hard - fought bout.

* * *

SUN, MOON & STARS

Sky is always lit up with their brightness both by day & night.
Innumerable as they are, yet, they don't
collide or in other words fight.
They just go on shining,
adding to nature's charm.
Caring for one 'n' other without
    Causing anyone any harm.
I don't understand, why don't
We, on our earth, behave that way!
Shine, live & let others live in peace each day!
We disturb ours & other's peace
without any worth-while reason in the
twinkling of an eye,
deceive, cheat, lie & behave as a sly.
Each one's life is as precious, as it is to a king.
Life is, as it is, tiresome. so, we all
must, hand in hand, together sing.
Our planet is shrinking with alarming
population growth rate.
That, basically causes crime, incivility,
savagery & teaming million's miserable fate.
To check it, is all in our hand
so that, everyone on our earth, has a house on a piece
of his own land
More mouths would lead to
less food & more ecological imbalance.
It's undoubtedly, for the whole
humanity, the most formidable challenge.

Sun, moon & stars, due to our planet's
pristine natural beauty, envy our mother earth.
By controlling birth rate, we
could easily protect & preserve
natural charms & serenity of
    our beautiful hearth!

* * *

TENSION - FREE LIFE

Tension is due to misdeeds,
like crops are due to their seeds.
Ill got, is generally, ill spent,
like, a tenant who ends up paying,
either voluntarily or by court order, eventually pays his rent.
We don't think before doing a wrong.
Thereafter, we keep hearing day in
and out sounds of danger bells and gong.
Even if, wrong remains unnoticed,
    one gets older faster.
Since, one doesn't have any longer
that privilege of having a free and natural laughter.
Tension free life alone, could be healthy.
one without anxiety & worry could only be really wealthy.
Going against established norms,
customs and rules for personal gains is a sure path leading to
enormous mental agony and pain.
Some, thus, due to accumulated stress, end up as insane.
Only, clean and right dealings
can keep you absolutely dry, even in incessant rain.
To me, everyone seems to live in a glass -house,
whenever, one's pants are down, on-lookers exclaim;
what a louse?
Even if, others don't see,
at least you know for sure, what you are.
That keeps on nagging and thus, all happiness of life,
you yourself mar.
Abide by rules, norms, customs
and have fair dealings.
Remember, in your old house, you can't remain
protected for long by only false ceilings!

* * *

LOUD NOISES OF STILL SILENCE

Fixed gaze of a Mother who has lost her son,
has deafening sounds;
worst than that one hears at the
dead of night from Jackals and Hounds.
Young widow's face in sad silence,
     produces such booms;
worst than that created by thousands of power looms.
Morose and tragedy-struck face of a
lad who's been orphaned, gives
     enormous deafening shriek;
like, wailing and crying sounds of sea
birds and animals in crude oil
filled creek.
Sad and hunger stuck lifeless eyes of
Mal-nutrition child, produce
awfully jarring note;
like, in a cemetery, in pitch dark night,
     big owl's hoot.
A helpless innocent's mute face
     has stunning sound; like that of a thunder-clap
right next to the ears.
I don't know why people's ears shy away from latent decibels of innocent's
tears.
If, all of us recognize and respect
     sounds of sad and grim silence,
we could perhaps, live with that
     requisite temperance and balance!

* * *

A WAY FOR SELF- IMPROVEMENT

True confession makes one feel light.
Coaxes thereafter, to do everything right.
Otherwise, guilt keeps bothering
both heart and mind.
It keeps eating up from within these vital
parts leaving absolutely sick behind.
If err is to human and forgive to divine,
Then, after committing a sin, it is moral
obligation to tell Him the
truth and seek His mercies and blessings benign.
Since, God is dealing with human
beings, He can possibly forgive you once or twice.
Don't expect Him to care for you if,
you keep repeating sin and reinforcing your vice.
It's a means to effect a dramatic
change of both heart and mind,
a practical way to convert your
savage psyche into a benevolent and kind.
Try it honestly, you may succeed.
Thereafter, to your inner voice, you've
to give due heed.
There's nothing wrong if you've committed a mistake.
Just make sure, you don't repeat
it for God's sake.

* * *

BIGGEST HUMAN FAILING

Some burn & some bury their dead.
While living, on such meaningless
    rituals, they lose their head.
Some have their national flag in
white & some in red.
Killing others across man-made dividing
line, is our national duty they said.
When will we understand that one who
kills & one who gets
killed are one God's own spark?
How long will we keep waiting for
skies to fall in order to catch a lark?
Other heavenly bodies
don't seem to have any life
whereas our planet has & looks so
marvelous from just outer space.
What a pity, on the same planet human
beings have hypocrisy, savagery & treachery
as their life's base!
We don't realize that these very
bacteria have wiped out, in our past, race after race.
Nothing has changed in reality except,
guns & lethal weapons have
replaced good old lance & mace.
It's high time, all of us; big
or small, rich or poor
bring about a radical change
    in our very outlook.
we've to put into practice, without any
colored interpretations, what's given in
    our respective most sacred book.

* * *

MAY BE, IT COULD HELP YOU!

We promised each other to
lovingly
share,
genuinely care,
breathe free air,
be honest and fair,
respectfully dare,
do religiously our daily prayer,
talk out our perceptions thread-bare,
go together up and down the life stair,
work out conscientiously to be a perfect pair,
and make our story unique and rare.
Also,
not to
snare,
split hair,
give stony stare,
avoid all life-less glare,
behave just like a horse and mare,
just live through life with only four legs; bare.
Our promise is still holding out
We would stick to it till our last no doubt.
Going by this unwritten and unsaid code,
have helped turn our small home into a heavenly abode.
You, too, could give it a sincere try.
I'm sure, you would only smile
throughout without a silent cry.

* * *

YOU DESERVE A BREAK

Day to day life chores make one's
   'life awfully busy,
so much so, that one often feels dizzy.
They say change of work and
routine has inherent rest,
still, one has to keep
always, a watch on sagging zeal and zest.
Life without interest and 'go'
tires one rather fast,
result is stress, strain and fatigue
which, doesn't let one last.
Therefore, off and on, one needs a break.
Sometimes, even for just 'heck of it' sake.
You must go out of your
house for enjoying a week end,
with people whom you love and
admire e.g. your wife, sons,
daughters and genuine friend.
It is a must to behave like
   a child or go crazy once a while.
Be cheerful and have a free and natural
laughter and always bear your charming smile.
During day, find some time to hear or
tell an anecdote.
Be romantic in your thoughts and keep riding
that life's fun boat.

During week days sometimes,
have a break and call up
someone who is dear.
Try and brave a pleasant
smile in your place of work for all far and near.
Don't you bother unnecessarily about,
what will people talk,
life, would then appear, a cake walk.

* * *

BE A MAN

Those, who, in moments of crisis,
    bite their nail,
in trying times, turn pale,
don't face up a gale,
& are always seen wagging
    their tail,
certainly, aren't worth
    being called a male.
Those, who, possess courage
    of conviction, are
    really great.
Greatest is he, who,
doesn't compromise it
    for any bait.
Some don't mind paying,
for calling spade a spade,
    any price,
Like a bread is to be
knifed in order to
    get a slice.
Life is worth living if
you bring courage into it.
Those, who, surrender,
lose honor too, in addition to
their lives with it.
People recall memories of those
who exhibited dauntless
courage with reverence.
Those who live and die with courage,
certainly deserve both
    friend's &foe's due deference.

* * *

MORALITY

Try and live with your head high,
if you, want to avoid a lot of
uncalled for pain and sigh.
I've seen many dying, many times
    before they actually die.
Believe you me, at that time then, there
is no one wishing
you respectfully a good bye.
You can keep your head
high only, if you keep self-respect intact,
it calls for putting your moral values
whatever, one does in effect.
Hypocrisy degrades one's character.
Remember, nothing remains hidden
    from our eternal benefactor.
We could tell a million lies to
others but not one to self.
With what face do we then,
seek at the fag-end, His blessings and help?
Some say morally speaking, what's
right and wrong must change with times.
Like fluctuating is, purchasing power
    of your dimes.
Truthfulness, steadfastness and self
esteem could only help you
keep head high with honor
        and dignity.

Otherwise, you could keep groping
    in dark till eternity.
All that is fine
But, I ask you one question; Have you seen a
lemon orchid owner selling
anything else except lime?

* * *

HOPE AND DESPAIR

Hope sustains life..
That's why, all over the world, every one
is waging struggle and putting up with
    strife.
It also, envisages in its fold, a lot
    of pain.
In the gap between expectation and
actuality, hinges whether one remains sane
    or turn insane.
Hope germinates optimism and in some, faith
    and confidence.
When these are belied, one gets unusually
    perturbed and tense.
Hope and despair are two faces of the
    same coin.
like, need to kill and killing instinct are
    synonymous of a lion
Without hope and expectation, there is no
    motivation.
State of mind breeds negative forces, inducing
    laziness and mental isolation.
Therefore, to reduce tension, one must
    harbor realistic hope.
Otherwise, stress and strain of life is rather
    hard to cope.

* * *

SILENCE AND SOLITUDE

It helps one to talk to Him and have His company.
It helps one to coordinate all His frequencies and
    create a melodious symphony.
In it, one can easily dive deep within and
      find out the cause and location of impurity and dirt.
After identification, remedial measures can be
    taken so that it may no longer cause disorder and hurt.
With it, one comes back to mother earth.
Believe me, with sincere practice, you'll realize even amidst
all noises and company, silence and solitude isn't in dearth.
It helps one feel one's own pulse and fathom
it's true strength.
Soon, one starts perceiving this otherwise,
unfathomable inner world's breadth and length..
In the initial stages of spiritual ascendency, It's a must.
Like, before tampering of Iron, one has to remove it's rust.
It helps stabilize one's mind,
by knocking off anger, passion, greed and helps turn one,
    serene and sublime.
It's pure Gold.
With its use, one can get self under a complete hold.
It's important for any worthwhile
spiritual communication.
Remember, for it, one doesn't have to give anyone a
    justification.
One can get it without singing a rhyme.
Therefore, how about initiating yourself into it,
without losing any more time!

* * *

DEMONS IN THE GARB OF SAINTS

When there was no religion on our earth, it was
    certainly better times.
At least in the name of religion,
various religious groups like, in.
these days, didn't indulge in
    dastardly and heinous crimes.
Everyone today, seems to try and get
by hook or crook name, powers and fame.
In its pursuit; they generally
    forget to have basic human shame.
After indulgence, offer excuses to
their own conscience which, are more than lame.
No one seems to put up a sincere hard-work.
Whereas, in discharging basic
duties towards world society,
everyone seems to shirk.
Minds in pursuit of worldly
    pleasures seem to have gone more
    than morbid and berserk.
Even, His occasional hard
blows, intended to make him mend his ways,
don't give him jolt and jerk.
In the garb of being an authority on
religion, men preach most irreligious things.
Get killed thousands of innocents with
their most venomous stings.
We should forget religion unless,
we understand truly why it exists,
and foster feelings of love, compassion
    and tolerance amidst.

* * *

TAKE A STEP

A time comes in everyone's life
when, one is required to take hard decision.
One has to address oneself then and
Concentrate on the problem and
    fathom pros and cons with precision.
As both horizontals and verticals make
    the picture complete,
One needs courage to venture out
    when darkness of night is dense and deep.
Many people's experience suggest that
those who, take the first step.
    generally never repent.
Come out of thousands of mallet
strokes without a dent.
Pre-requisite to success is to have a clear vision.
Take help of your inner strength for
    that vital decision.
Having done that, one has to set
    a practical goal. Thereafter, in the pursuit
of its achievement, put in his heart and soul.
All difficulties and problems en-route,
    have their own cure.
Dedication, sincerity and devotion to
the cause, for any meaningful success, have to be there for sure.
Some moments in life pose a
    great challenge.
Epitome of maturity and confidence
lies in accepting them with a smile
    without losing balance.

Remember,. life isn't a bed of roses,
One who remains indecisive
or doesn't take timely decision, finally loses.
One is defeated when one, gives up.
Therefore, one has to relentlessly & resolutely
keep trying & Not to 'Give up'.

* * *

THIN DIVIDING LINE

Really, thin is the line between sanity & insanity.
Collective sanity brings happiness
& prosperity, whereas, insanity,
    enormous sufferings to all humanity.
Naughty demon in us, induces
everyone to do something against established norm.
Cunningly curtains at that time,
    all anticipated nerve wrecking jolts & storms.
Man at that point of time, forgets to hear the inner voice.
Obviously then, what is convenient &
self pleasing, is his choice.
To his horror, he realizes soon,
    that nothing remains hidden.
We then, remain worried & consumed
by the guilt of doing something which was forbidden.
So much so that, one, doesn't get sleep,
then all monsters, snakes, scorpions &
great spiders, in slumber, along with him creep.
Remains restless and loses weight due to fear
    of what may follow.
Thus, age goes by & man remains coward, shallow & hollow.
Therefore, remedy lies in nipping the evil in Its bud,
Wisdom lies in finding a way which avoids mud.
Hence, one has to listen to inner promptings when cunning mind is about to
dominate.
And thus, help make a promising future
    & better fae.

* * *

DECISION MAKING & THEREAFTER

Unless you admit, acknowledge & pause,
how can you hope to get at the real cause?
Any live situation merits understanding the verticals
and horizontals, as then alone, a worth- while picture
      would probably emerge,
otherwise, it would remain unperceivable, lop-sided
or veiled behind a surge.
Application of common sense, logic & experience
would then, help you weigh various pros & cons.
Remember, you can hope to tame a bull only, when,
you hold him by his horns.
Decision has to be timely and sound.
otherwise, any project may not even take off ground.
Once, you've reached a decision,
you must go full steam.
Keep your eyes &.
ears open as you go along
and don't you get into a day dream.
Application of correction is more than vital
like, ascribing a poem, its apt title.
You would encounter challenges, both pseudo & formidable.
Keep your wits cool & intact without being brash & irritable.
Don't blame anyone, even, luck for a failure and keep cribbing.
Sometimes, goal isn't scored, as there had been
too much of unnecessary dribbling.
Success in any venture is sum total of everything put in including
'General Luck'

Remember, sometimes even world first class cricketers,
get out at 'duck.'
Those, who arrive at decisions & act,
find themselves certainly better than indecisive ones, in-fact.
Success, in no way, should swell up your head.
If it's so, you're as good as living dead.

* * *

PERSEVERANCE & PATIENCE

Like a spring, beginning of all big things is rather small.
Like everyone before walking, learns to crawl.
Like a rain drop is very much part of an ocean.
Soul of every living being is, in essence, the same one
God in motion.
It descends into & ascends out of any one, at His will.
Rest is all a mere common story of someone in a typical mill.
We forget that this Universe for its present
	existence has taken billions of years.
Spirit & Cultural heritage of any race is outcome of
cumulative efforts of countless philosophers, thinkers, sages &. seers.
Like construction of a house takes time,
	while it's destruction, comparatively nil.
In happiness, times fly while in despair, it stands still.
Those, who aspire to get to dizzy, heights in the twinkling
	of an eye, obviously live in fool's paradise.
Only, those who believe in 'Slow & Steady wins the
	race' are undoubtedly wise.
Those, who are sincere about their goal,
	burn midnight oil while, their agers sleep.
When you lose sight of the very aim, you can land up in trouble;
	sometimes, unmanageable & deep.
Genuine efforts & patience alone,
can ensure tranquility of mind.
Remember, after testing you alone,
would He be benevolent & kind!

* * *

HUMOROUS APPROACH

Humor in life comes out of
positive approach, wit & wisdom.
It's a sure way to kill emptiness
disinterest & boredom.
Those, who receive its daily dose,
are able to face this world
    with a straight nose.
Through humor, one can
    soften the hard blows of life,
with laughter, heart remains
tension - free though out hard moments
    of strife.
Remember, laughter reduces mental
    distance between
even worst of foes.
you would know, quite funny is the
Link between one's heels & toes.
It's a skill, that one can acquire, with ease.
After acquisition, nurturing it,
would bring in your life, real peace.
Through laughter alone, you
could survive the most painful
    situation,
like, any written expression would
become meaningful only after,
application of right kind of
    punctuation.

Laughter is a barometer of
    general health.
It just can't be compensated
    by worldly riches or wealth.
We're here for an unpredictable spell.
So, how about laughing a while!
Therefore, rather than anger, let the laughter
stir up your bile!

* * *

KEEP YOUR KITES FLYING

In my childhood, kite flying
    was more than an obsession,
I used to dream about in my
class-rooms about the evening session.
It was my ardent dream to be
    the best in kite-flying.
Obviously, it required expert hands
& real professional & business like buying.
I realized whenever, my thread was
weak & full of knots,
I lost my kites by the dozen &
was laughing stock of even tiny tots..
With frail thread, kite couldn't
remain intact due to
    blows of strong breeze,
light & small kites would,
    with those gushes, just freeze.
Now, I realize how true it is to life!
Knotty twisted, and weak characters,
can't brave rough times and put up with-strife.
Kite of life, soon gets severed.
Thereafter, drifts away in a manner;
    uncontrolled & weird.
So, if keeping your life-kite up, above all,
    is your exciting quest,
Remember, thread of strong & formidable character is
    the best bet.!

* * *

POSITIVITY IN LIFE

I get fascinated when I behold;
On a tree, squirrels playing hide & seek,
mother bird back on her nest with an
insect in her beak,
team of climbers with their flag right
    on top of a virgin peak.
Ants sharing a mammoth weight,
Crocodile rocking tongue as a bait,
Tiger next to a water point, hiding in wait,
young one awaiting impatiently for his date.
Amidst murky mud, a full bloom lotus flower,
upon dry & hot sand dune, a torrential shower,
On a historical battlefield a victory tower.
Honey Bee's devotion towards the Queen Bee,
dexterous hands in gardens plucking tea,
unflinching determination of explorers
braving a mighty sea.
Pet Dog's faithfulness & devotion,
Peacock's dance sequence & majestic motion.
Beaming & radiant face of someone returning home with promotion.
Soldiers fighting their way into enemy lines,
newly born calf, before walking, stumbling on hoofs many a time,
mountain slopes studded with rows of pines.
Infant's expression on the sight of his mother,
about grown up sister, the concerned looks of a big brother.
Mother Teresa's feelings on the sufferings of other.

Rain and sun together, falling on a patch,
Team's hugs & kisses to the player who was
    instrumental in winning a tough fought match,
expressions of a fisherman on
    realization of his unimaginable catch.
I, also, get fascinated with the ups & downs of life.
My fascination propels me to cope up smilingly,
with the privations and sufferings
    which are, more than rife.

* * *

FEAR & REMEDY

Like 'Static' effects any Radio receptions,
so does fear, which, effects any mind's perceptions.
Fear is constructive
as well as destructive.
It comes from heart & grips the whole body.
It disturbs heart's rhythm altogether & then all
    actions become rather shoddy.
Consciousness of pain based on own & other's
experiences, causes anxiety & fear.
When the same gets unbridled, it leads to
    shedding many a tear.
Fear paralyses both nerves & will,
motivation, morale, and
    spirits then mercilessly it would kill.
Exhibition of Cautious fear however, is being wise.
Whereas, unreasonable one, brings along avoidable
    sufferings in its guise.
Generally, we suffer from anxiety & worry even
    before the malady has come.
Shun the very thought that anything could be
    so fearsome.
Take your heart & mind away from the subject
    which causes fear.
Think of Him, seek His benign protection & soon
    His foot-steps you'll hear.
Remember, timid & weak-hearted one dies each
    day a number of time.
Surrender to unmanliness is unbecoming
    & in-fact, against self, a crime.

* * *

YOU CAN DO IT

Extremes of anything & everything are bad,
end result then, is bound to be sad.
One can't afford to lose inner rhythm & balance
in any pursuit.
Remember, even a plant grows both upwards by way of stem.
branches, leaves & downwards as it's root.
Extreme mental involvement causes mental fatigue
& ill health.
There is no compensation for the same even,
by any amount of wealth.
Similarly, extreme physical activity can be instrumental
in effecting a permanent physical harm.
Only, application of moderation in thought and deed,
would prove to be a soothing balm.
Temperance ensures stability of both mind & body,
Also, actions don't ever turn out to be shoddy.
It's something, that is very much a practical
reality.
By its application, everyone is likely to succeed
in overall totality.
It is a magic word, which also induces
virtues of patience, forbearance & fortitude.
With it, one could sail through a great range of
altitude.

* * *

OPTIMISM

NEW HORIZONS

In our mountains, there's always yet another hill.
Somewhere, on this beautiful earth of ours,
a terrorist awaits for another kill.
In our deserts, there's always yet another dune.
Somewhere, on this lovely earth of ours,
someone is misusing His blessings and boon.
In our sky, there is always yet another star.
Somewhere, on this fascinating earth of ours, an addict is
searching yet another drug joint and a bar.
Over our seas, there's always yet another tide.
Somewhere, on this magnificent earth of ours,
someone's sister or daughter is being
compelled to commit suicide.
In our grazing lands, there's always yet another green grass blade.
Somewhere, on this fantastic earth of ours,
a sex-maniac is planning to rape a young maid.
In our fertile minds, there's always yet another thought.
Somewhere, on this charming world of ours
someone is laughing at someone else's cost.
In our oceans, there's always yet another under current.
somewhere, on this marvelous world of ours,
dead body of a hapless and innocent is being secretly burnt.
In the field of weaponry, there's always yet another gun.
Somewhere, on this enchanting world of ours,
a mother sheds silent tears on barbaric
and cold blooded murder of her innocent son.
In our metropolitan cities, there's always yet another lane.
Somewhere, on magically alluring world of ours,
someone steals and murders another
for want of a grain.

Amidst valleys and mountains, there's
always yet another picturesque sight.
Somewhere, on this attractive world of ours,
someone is being choked since, he dared
to clamor for his & others basic birth right.
In en-catchment areas, there is always yet another brook:
Somewhere, on this superb earth of ours, someone is devising new ways
and means to cheat and crook.
If somehow, these negative forces on our
beautiful earth of ours, vanish or go underground,
There would be real peace, happiness and prosperity all around.!

* * *

OUR PLANET TURNS INTO PARADISE

No one remembers Him when the going is good,
whereas, everyone should.
Everyone remembers only Him when the spirits are dim.
It just shows how selfish we are right up to our brim.
Remember Him and sing Thy praises since in Him alone,
ultimate truth lies.
He alone could show all the way to paradise.
We're all His spark.,
Alas! we keep groping in dark.
Aimlessly we wander and seek physical pleasure.
Don't bother to fathom the inner voice by any measure.
Since, we keep loving ourselves and not His creation,
the end result is enormous misery and frustration.
The panacea of all ills lies in selfless love like, that of a mother.
The pleasure and solace that one derives out of it lies in no other.
Love is the language of soul.
It encompasses humane, kind and benevolent actions
for His creation as a whole.
It's the key to salvation.
The only way for anyone's immortalization.
The true practice of this magical
four letter word 'love', could only save this planet.
Since, all religions of world have this as their basic tenet.
He is with you with His limitless love at all times.
Why don't you shun hatred, jealousy, anger, pride
and egoism and help make our planet devoid of all crimes?
Sooner you realize, better it is.
That's the only way to reinforce and spread His bliss!

* * *

ONE HUMANITY, ONE EARTH

East or West, North or South, all places are
    after all, on our one earth.
Where, each one of us, has somewhere or the other,
    his hearth.
Native place has no doubt, it's own attractions;
where, there is a deep sense of belonging &
    spontaneous natural affectionate reactions,
& where, having come back, one finds not much has changed.
Yet, there are some places on the same earth,
where prevailing environments make you behave like,
    most unnatural as if, deranged.
If, all of us adopt our beautiful planet
    & call it our native place,
the attitude itself, could be instrumental in getting
    some 'solace.
All of us have to have, feelings for the
    oppressed, Where ever they be.
because, for the concept of universal brotherhood,
    it alone, has the key.
I wonder, why don't we all stir up when natural
    calamities like volcanoes, typhoons, quakes,
    famine & epidemics take a heavy
toll of our brothers & sisters anywhere on our planet!
Why don't we all have, to govern our affairs, one humane senate?
It's high time world over, towards this end, all of us
    should show our collective will &inclination.

Without which, as time goes by, our narrow & parochial
vested interests would keep on reinforcing our hesitation.
The ethos of genuinely caring for one another, regardless
of man-made barriers, has to be fundamentally at the bottom line.
Otherwise, hypocrisy & affectation would only
add to suffering for all of us & manifest into real
  bad time!

      * * *

MAN AND HIS RELIGION

All religions of the world in essence, are manifestations of truth
and speak only universal peace and brotherhood of mankind.
All saints and seers through ages, spoke pure dictates
of their conscience and coaxed their followers to bury their differences
behind.
Religions are analogous to various streams with a common
destination; the ocean of fantasy and eternal joy,
but, unfortunately, the history of mankind along with
development of various religions had been a story of
barbarism, cruelty and innumerable one's hue and cry.
The followers of various religions, over the annals
of history, had been most irreligious.
As, for most of them, not ends, but means were dear
and prestigious.
Past has witnessed mass blood-shed and cruelty by
irreligious followers in the name of religion.
Present is just a continuation of that past with more
complicated and complex delusions.
Those irreligious people have adorned the garb of a
Capitalist and Communist in present times.
They don't kill, don't betray as they profess but, it's
because of their silent approval, there exists
on our earth killings, betrayals and brutal savage crimes.
Both speak volumes on the basic freedom of everyone
and his birth right to live.
Yet, both dictate others how to breathe and what to give.
In recent years, the thread that holds the cursed
sword of Damocles over mankind has grown still hinner,
Prospects of universal peace; the most precious thing, have become still
dimmer.

Like in past, we failed to comprehend that the life
of a Muslim, Hindu or a Christian is equal,
In present times, the same scenario exists between
a capitalist and a communist which is equally
grim and fatal.
Today, the threat of world-wide conflagration hangs,
regardless of political and religious views over all mankind, since the means
to achieve peace aren't honest
and, therefore, this confused state of mind.
The only thing we can truly give our children is peace
and that's why, millions of people throughout the world,
are conducting a relentless struggle.
A dispassionate look on the verticals and horizontals
of the problem of promotion and preservation of
world peace is worth the trouble.
World spends a million dollar every minute on
stockpiling of arms.
While, thirty children die of poverty malnutrition and starvation.
It's the most brutal paradox of our times with its
ugly manifestation.
How can a dialogue with a base of hypocrisy
motivated by malice bear fruit?
When both due to distrust, jealousy and hatred keep
their nuclear warheads aimed and all set to shoot?
Both think, keeping the fate of entire humanity to
ransom is an expression of their superiority and
National chauvinism.
But, they don't realize that after a holocaust,
even the most convinced ideologue will be unable to
distinguish the ashes of capitalism from that of Communism.

Wars are complete knock - down of collective
human wisdom;
warring nations get collectively busy in adding new
dimensions for mass - killings inside the enemy's kingdom
what a paradox the so called civilized in a war does his best to prove
to be in his worst.
And, doesn't bother or hesitate to do any heinous, cruel,
barbaric or savage crime before mingling with his dust!
It's strange that man has reached moon but,
Hasn't achieved peace for all.
Civilization, may it be expressed in
any language, prompts people
of world society to make life more meaningful without a brawl.
A viable peace can only rein if, everyone on the
face of our earth, is peaceful.
Back to square one, I'm convinced, it's religion again,
which can make it feasible.
Truth is reality, reality God,
God purity and from purity comes feeling.
It's religion, the truthful understanding and practice
of which, alone, can give, at the moment, the required
touch of healing.
Let us· all put into practice our religions
in letter and spirit, sink our differences and help
suffering humanity with all our mite!
Let us all kindle the torch of universal peace
and brotherhood and help make our world full
of sun-shine and bright!
If, we forget to do it today, it'll certainly
be too late.
Our earth will nose-dive into dark,
lifeless, frozen and horrible fate.

If, we do what our inner promptings and rhythms goad,
we'll remove the nuclear war psychosis
which, looms large over the young generation like a million ton load.
By following the religion of universal peace, love and brotherhood,
everyone will add to the quality and objectivity of life.
Coming generations, will then, blossom without any
fear or unwarranted anxiety, worry and strife.
Don't our children deserve such a present from all of us?
Well! if that be so, shouldn't we hurry up?
I think, true expression of our love and affection towards
them should be, to make a sincere and
concerted effort for world peace and
NOT TO GIVE UP!

* * *

WONDERFUL WINDOWS

I see this world through my yes,
perceive all truths and lies.
I opened them as I slipped out of mother's womb,
Would need someone's help to shut them
on the day of doom.
My eyes are inquisitive to see and learn more and more.
Even in deep slumber, I keep sketching behind closed door.
These are most magnificent windows of mind.
Their preciousness can only be evaluated by a blind.
Sometimes, I see things unbelievable,
sharpness of images on mind, absolutely incredible.
They help me formulate my life philosophy.
Coupled with inner wisdom, coax me
proclaim sometimes, a prophecy.
Blessed are those who, through them, form only good and positive images.
Upon how charming are the eyes on a face, that the beauty and personality
hinges.
Through them, I express both love and anger,
Differentiate clearly feminine from a gander.
Bright and sparkling
eyes denote sun-shine.
Truthful & loyal ones are unusually sublime.
True patriot's eyes have a distinct glow.
A terrorist cast on any onlooker, a murderous blow.
Eyes speak volumes of one's character,
guide us like any play by its director.
If you make your eyes good, you'll see only goodness.
If you let them go berserk, you'll experience
only tremors of brute rudeness.

Eyes also, express shock and grief sometimes, with and
sometimes without tears.
Through them, unsaid messages are
picked up by saints and seers.
How about using them for seeing and doing good?
I'm sure at least that much all of us could!

* * *

DARK DAYS WOULD SOON BE OVER

Moonless night,
gives me a fright.
shooting stars and owl's stare,
gives me unusual scare.
Shadow less trees
    make me tense.
Lonely stretches discolor & disfigure
    my common sense.
I hear unusual sounds
    of agony and pain.
Fear haunts me in an
    unknown lane.
Jet black darkness on ground,
makes my heart pound.
All faces appear to be those of hungry hound.
Stars; big & small appear to
    scoff & jeer.
I hear jackal's howling
    & dog's wailing far and near.
Darkness of still night
    dampens my heart and mind.
I get a strange feeling as if,
I'm being chased & someone is getting closer to me from behind.
Uncanny silence makes my
    senses weird
    & spirits depressed.
Out in the open, I feel as if, an
    orphan; oppressed.

Yet, I see through dark & stark
times since, I know there would
     soon be a moon lit night.
My eyes would then feast on majestic
peaceful and soothing sight.
In full moon's benign light,
everything would turn out
     to be just right.
I love thee oh, my moon!
Please show up & dispel
     darkness around me soon.

* * *

SILVER LINING

Times are blissfully changing for better.
Realization of respect for human beings,
their rights, dignity and thoughts is the crux of the matter.
Bitter enemies of past have now a fair
      chance to shake hands.
There seems now, a viable possibility of
having one humane world government for all lands.
      We've to collectively think ways and.
means to stop Acid-rain.
Provide one 'n' all a shelter, clothes and adequate grain.
We've to ensure that Green-house
effect doesn't become a reality.
Spectrum and quality of life, for all on the globe,
has to be collectively reviewed by all scientists,
engineers and doctors in its totality.
We've to ensure that meteoroids and asteroids
from outer space don't collide
      with our earth and cause thousands
of N Bomb worth a bang.
For that, all our engineers and space scientists
have to put their heads together as members of one gang.
Hand in hand, we've to fight all kinds of viruses and disease.
Like, as batsmen, we've to ensure that
we remain as if a 'live wire' on the crease.
Our young generation could then, blossom
in complete freedom without any fears.
Instead of tears and cries then, there would be
      only laughs and cheers.

Obnoxious looking war tools and implements
could be used collectively for the good of human race,
Blissful peace then, could reign on both our
    planet and space.
We could easily channelize all our energies
for peace, preservation and prosperity of all mankind.
Forget our bitter past history and leave it far behind.
Life in the lap of bountiful nature with all
our materialistic and spiritual advancements,
would be a real fun.
One earth, one moon, one human race without
any color, religion, caste and creed and nationality
under one great Sun!
If we preserve our nature and its resources are
    shared by all,
      We won't have 'Haves' and 'Have Not's and thus,
everyone on the face of our earth, will have
    a royal ball.
It's very much possible if, all of us take
    bold initiatives and
collective steps in right earnest.
All of us, have to, for attainment of this noble goal,
    turn absolutely honest.

* * *

WHISPERING BREEZE

Pick up my whisper, as,
    for you, it's a great message.
You seem to need it like an
    open wound requires a bandage.
I've travailed through distant
lands and passed by many people;
both strong and feeble.
All sleuthed in ignorance and
    drenched in cosmic delusions,
in a great mess & amidst all kinds of confusions,
Almost all are causing to themselves by their actions, self-embarrassment.
Obviously, it's an avoidable self harassment.
Their selfish and short sighted pursuits day in and out, fetch some transitory
happiness but, in essence enormous misery.
All seem to be adding most sad and
unfortunate chapters to their collective history.
Grim silence and worries on their
faces, show amply that they aren't at ease
Since, their brains are working
Overtime in negative directions,
they cause disturbance to their own as well, as other's peace.
Peace, both inside and outside is
Most invaluable and for real
happiness an absolute necessity.
Like, a strict watch on diet and adequate physical
exercise, to control obesity.
My whispering campaign so far,
hasn't had desired result.
However, I'd go on in order to
save you from worries, embarrassment and insult.

* * *

WORLD WITH A DIFFERENCE

Take me into that exclusive world,
where reigns only love and nothing else,
where, even if, one wants to, can't become tense.
Lead me to that place, where, from you, there is no separation,
& where, there is natural spontaneity without any hesitation.
Guide me to that destination where, my eyes behold only You,
where, basic human compassions are a reality without any one's hue.
Show me the way for that great reunion,
where, lovable expressions and impressions are not just notional intuition.
I crave for only that destination, where You await.
What a pity, even my sixth sense doesn't prompt that blessed date!
At the moment, I'm piloting my own aircraft,
whereby, I could, at will, decide own course.
I could pick up even your coded messages sent on Morse.
Don't you think, it would be too late, when fuel runs out.
then, I won't get any meaningful help even if, I cry or shout!
Therefore, time is now, when, I'm still in command.
Rest assured, that's my only life-time demand.

* * *

PRESERVATION OF HUMANITY

Slender is the thread between sanity and insanity,
both are immensely innate in all humanity.
There are some who, understand what their conscience
    dictates and act in time.
There are others who, defy inner voice &
    bend towards crime.
One who listens, may outwardly suffer but,
    possesses inner peace and real pleasure.
The other remains spiritually bankrupt although,
    amidst abundant worldly treasure.
Some plants give fascinating flowers even amidst
    scum and dirt.
Whereas some, even amidst expert hands, cause
    displeasure and hurt.
Experience of all man-kind abundantly proves that love is
    epitome of all civility.
It generates fellow feelings of respect for all and virtue of humility.
Without which, life seems moron and dull
like, a rust-eaten ship-hull.
No one, except oneself, can help in this respect anybody.
Otherwise, the whole life becomes shoddy.
Genuine and selfless love alone, is panacea for
    all ills plaguing our world today.
otherwise, all of us, would one day, through a bloody nose, pay.

* * *

MATERIALISM

A COSMIC DELUSION

Hi, I am money!
Through me, you get shelter, clothes and taste foods and honey.
When I'm in abundance, you squander.
When I'm at premium, ways and means you ponder.
All comforts and pleasures are accessible when I'm with thee.
Life is agony, frustration and a curse without me.
You only aim to earn,
whereas, I make you slowly burn.
You try both honest and dishonest means to possess.
I've made your life just a game of chess.
In order to get me, you stage struggle and read.
I make you engrossed life-long in counting your bead.
My tingling sound on slot machines seems
heavenly and fascinating.
My appreciation and depreciation at stock exchange
    is alluring and exciting.
When I show up you clamor for more.
When I don't, better fate you implore.
Some of you, keep devising ways and
    means to make quick buck.
Some of you, pay obeisance to
    God to please Him for good luck.
My friendship and annoyance makes you experience
    heaven and hell.
For me, even some, their self respect & honor, sell.
You visit stock markets, gambling dens, race courses
    as behind the curtain, I lure.
It's because of me, the world is classified as rich,
middleman and poor.
You find me in currency notes, precious stones,
    coins and gold.

Without me, you look tired and soon get old.
Some of you, win me by cheating,
Strangely enough, most of you call me fleeting.
If I make you feel on top of the world, I also,
     don't let you sleep.
Through me, reward for your luck, innovation,
          sense of courage and perseverance, you reap.
My force compels you to value time.
In my dragnet, world witnesses all sorts of crime.
For me, you have an unending desire.
For want of me, poor throw their dead in rivers
     as, they Can't afford to light a pyre.
Your entire life is virtually devoted to me.
Yet, I ditch you at your end and don't go with thee!

* * *

STRUGGLE FOR REAL FREEDOM

Where is my freedom gone
with which, I was born?
Over the years, instead of consolidating, I lost it and became a slave;
of egoism, lust, greed, pride, anger, jealousy and hate.
I may appear to some influential and rich
but, my slavery has made me spiritually a pauper.
So, I'll go through the rut most unnoticed
like on grass, a grass hopper.
I realize materialism is the root cause of this wretched state.
The realization itself, is undoubtedly rather late.
These forces have held me firmly in their
yoke and I'm left with a little time.
Towards my own soul, I've done a lot of crime.
Their target area is conscience which, is attacked
overwhelmingly from all directions.
Once penetrated, it gets extremely difficult to
offer meaningful resistance.
Materialism injects want,
desire and crave.
These forces then, overpower
conscience and make anyone a nit-wit and naive.
Remedy lies in a relentless struggle
against the shackles of this worst form of slavery.
Thus, one can give oneself a good account of real bravery.
Will I die the death of a slave or will I be free
like, when I was born?
Will I be able to get a hold on my conscience
or will it remain life-long totally torn?

* * *

COSMIC MIRAGES

All seem to have their
    hearts set on cosmic delusions.
That's why perhaps, they're amidst
    hitherto unknown confusions.
For example, for some, love for their
heart-throb is a serious stuff,
whereas, she considers it a mere yet
    another game.
This kind of response to their
sentiments sometimes, make
    them forget even their own name.
For some, love for worldly possessions
force their brains work overtime.
When things don't go their way,
they turn under compulsions, rather unusually sublime.
For some, affections for their own kith and kin, lure
them do all sorts of things,
but, their behavior in return,
sometimes, makes them feel
as if, they've been injected with poison from
    innumerable venomous stings.
For some, money and it's collection,
seem to be the be all and end all of their lives,
when it ditches them or when
they have to leave it for their
final destination, makes them heave deep sighs.
For some, good eating, drinking
    and making merry seem to be
    the only life's goal,
when the same cause serious physical
ailments, they get a life time jolt.

For some, religion is a mere source of good living and
    wielding a real power,
when it's revealed to others, their rest of lives turn very bitter and sour.
To me, almost everyone seems to be sleuthed in
    abject ignorance despite,
        variety of educations.
Cosmic delusions for most, are undoubtedly
sources of heart failures, paralytic
strokes and complete breakdown of their nervous systems.

* * *

DEADLY SPIDERS OF MATERIALISM

Materialistic world is like an extremely
alluring and fascinating cobweb.
Once entangled, miseries,
sufferings and privations have no ebb.
Deadly spider of hatred, makes
one believe in maxim of 'Self,
    Before Service.'
For this spider,
all attempts of pray to break shackles of web are that
    of a novice.
Poisonous spider of anger forces one to try and
snap the strings of web with great fury and ferocity. Before spider approaches
it's pray,
it has got tired and resigns itself
to impending fate with strange curiosity.
Venomous poison of pride,
makes one get stuck, right
    next to the spider.
It's plight is like, racing
horse almost at the end of the race,
    without rider.
Horrible spider of greed,
makes one enter deep in web's funnel.
The pray doesn't know how to
    reverse at the end of the tunnel.
Terrible spider of ego is
    quick to grab it's pray,
with deadly sting, knocks of latter's
    light of the day.

In the cob-web of harmful spider of lust,
pray keeps on trying to free itself,
till it's dead due to fatigue & exhaustion.
Fact of materialistic life is, that
these webs are anywhere and
everywhere if you don't pay
  heed to inner word of caution.
Live in this world and enjoy it within
the limits of civility.
Remain tuned to Him, listen to inner
voice and shun all kinds of
  deviltry.

* * *

MY FLESH IS ON SALE

I've seen all kinds of male.
All of them, leave behind many a tell tale.
Some, novices visit to learn the game.
Some, live through the moments with that
    latent shame.
Some, pose boisterous & some turn pale,
due to lurking fear of landing
    up in jail.
Some, go on in a indiscreet somewhat, revengeful manner.
Some, bring with them that deceitful ardent lover's banner.
Some, try many a trick.
Sight of some, make me more than sick.
Some, are quick and some under drug influence,
    painfully slow.
With some, time somehow passes but, to some,
    I feel like kicking with my toe.
Some, leave with a sense of distinct guilt &
some, with a strange sense of achievement.
Some, happily pay up and some, try ending up
    with mere verbal appeasement.
Outside my four walls, they don't recognize.
Whereas, on my bunk, the regular one's
    denounce their very wives.
Some wretched, insist that I lie bare
    & for some, it doesn't matter.
Some are quiet workers & some prefer to chatter.
They don't realize that for me, it's just a matter
    of painful routine.
As, I've been forced into it, in male dominated
society which is, incredibly unscrupulous,
    cunning & mean.

All consider me to be only a sex machine,
    available on coins, at will.
When on wrong side of youth, my value in market
depreciates nose dive like that-of a barren hill.
My youthful days alone, can ensure my food
    when I'm not worth a glance.
Therefore, I'm forced to work overtime & don't
    dare to lose a chance.
I know very well men from all walks of
    life & of all ages.
I find it very amusing, when I see these very
    men behaving in society like, sages.
No one cares for my emotions, fears &
    aspirations.
Whereas, everyone craves for maximum
return of their coins in a mood of strange
    celebrations.
During the act, I am as cold as dead.
Yet, most play strange games on my bed.
I see no way to my emancipation.
I see no end to my privation.
My flesh is on sale!

* * *

LOVE OF LIFE

Life is a great mystery,
like, unknown period of any history.
It takes you to strange people in
     unknown lands,
it makes you either shake or spurn hands.
It unfolds itself into hitherto unknown.
Strange enough, everyone comes in, walks through
& goes out absolutely alone.
It makes you witness strange things.
Makes you feel sometimes poorest of all &
sometimes king of kings.
Beauty lies undoubtedly, in not knowing what
     lies ahead.
If one knows, it'd be as good or bad as like,
     living dead.
One ought to accept thanking,
     what comes by, as it unfold.
Since, there is no way one could grip
     time & hold.
Cosmic delusions make all dance in many a
     strange step & great combinations.
If accompanying music is scintillating, you
love to be on floor, otherwise, get hallucinations.
Genuine interest in life is precious & a must.
Otherwise, anytime, this life- balloon can get burst.
Therefore, love it & respect it.
Otherwise, be prepared to pack up
any time your bags & kit.

* * *

DUNES OF LOVE

Love has many a form;
Under its extreme pressure, mind experiences
    many a tempest & storm.
Love for opposite sex is but natural,
traumatic experiences of heart-broken are
    more than pathetic & terrible.
A genuine lover in order to get his heart-throb,
    holds no bar.
That's why they say 'all is fair in love & war'.
In deep & desperate love, one can go mad.
Life stories of love torn & love lost are
    unusually tragic & sad.
Love for money is a gift of modern
    materialistic world.
In its pursuit, mind keeps on spinning
like a churning rotor in Curd.
Latter turns Curd into butter milk.
& former makes one forget even wear silk.
For some, loving body & its comforts is,
    life's sole aim,
In over luxury, it soon gets crippled &
    maimed.
There are some who, selflessly love
    suffering humanity, although are very rare,
joyfully other's sufferings & own smiles,
    with others, they share.
They alone, undoubtedly deserve God's choicest
      blessings & His benign personal care.
This form of love is the best amongst all.
He's unquestionably the greatest who,
remains engulfed in it, till his final call!

* * *

THIS WORLD IS A PLAY FIELD

I find almost everyone on the face of
our earth, playing games,
of course, under different names.
Some play in teams & some alone.
Any way, it doesn't matter as,
All are similar in their texture & tone.
Some follow unscrupulous but,
accepted rules & some, devise their own.
But, all aim to extract blood & sweat
    of others; both known & unknown.
Those, who think about their games as
totally Original are sadly mistaken.
As our ancestors also, knew
    tastes of Ham & Bacon.
At the end of these games, some become delirious but,
    experience transitory delights.
Soon to realize, that, only on empty &
meaningless aims had they focused,
    life long, their sights.
It's important & pertinent to ask
self a question; Towards pristine nature
& humanity, what's my contribution?
If, an honest answer is nil then,
rest assured, God would feel sorry
for affording you a unique chance
to be part of His incredibly
    fascinating creation!

* * *

CAN ANY ONE TELL ME?

Honey bees go on collecting
nectar from a common flower,
   without a fight.
Man goes on disturbing own
and other's peace day and night.
   I don't know why!
Parrots, after days hard labor,
get back home together, chirping merrily all the way.
If man could help it; after
dividing land and sky, he would even divide benign Sun's ray.
   I don't know why!
Birds, generally respect their
elders and follow them in perfect formation.
Some men, because of their skin color,
race or riches call themselves a superior creation.
   I don't know why!
Ants perform their
   duty most sincerely and run up in a straight line,
following a beaten track.
For selfish petty ends, even civilized men's personal
defense crack.
I don't know why!
Animals drink water from a common source without a brawl.
Men, states and countries over the same issue,
pounce at each other's throat and prowl
I don't know why!
Trees grow in nearness, hugging and kissing each other's leaves in
   perfect neighborhood.

Man, only knows how to sermonize and preach
    Universal brotherhood.
    I don't know why!
Love birds are most sincere to each other and
    die in separation.
Men through illicit & forbidden sex, seek
    thrill and elation.
    I don't know why!

* * *

SHUTTLE GAME

Like, a shuttle cock gets knocked by two players
across a net until, it has a weird flight.
So is, in this materialistic world, any man's plight.
He gets shuttled between players of his conscience on one side
and that of ego, hatred, greed, anger and pride
    on the other.
Game starts right from the time he partakes the
    lap of his mother.
He purposely bends rules of the game in
favour of one for selfish materialistic
gains and makes him win.
In the process however, he doesn't realize that
    he keeps on committing sin after sin.
He demoralizes the player of conscience right in the
beginning by having a tacit understanding with
self disguised as referee and spectators.
Lets other's score go up with those deceitful,
    camouflaged and concealed unsporting baiters.
Player of conscience tries his level best despite, heavy odds.
But, gets frustrated under spell of his
opponent's deceptive drops and shots.
A time comes when, it's entirely one sided game.
Player of ego, greed, hatred, anger and pride establishes supremacy,_
credibility and picks up name and fame.
Nevertheless, game goes on in man's mind
until, player of conscience, in utter disgust,
walks out of the ground.
Demoralized, dejected and frustrated without a crib or a sound.

By then, like a badly battered shuttle,
man's thoughts display that weird and wicked flight.
Loses that discretion of differentiating between
a wrong and right.
If, he were unbiased and sensible right from the
start, when score board showed
'Love Each'
surely, spiritual dizzy heights within his
life-time, were well within his reach.!

* * *

ANGER

In anger, the demon in you, takes over. Your expressions & actions then,
make You like a hot - air blower.
When you lose temper, you lose logic.
When you blow up, you lose your personality's charm & magic.
How illogical is it to think that,
everything around you should
move the way you like!
Better would be to keep cool &
mend own psyche.
Anger disturbs your rhythm & beat.
It upsets & unhinges your brain cells
from their natural seat.
Heat generated disturbs own as well
     as other's peace.
In exasperation, thinking ability
is the first casualty as brain comes.
     under a great siege.
It's a fallacy to think that your
anger would fetch desired result.
Imagine what'll happen if everyone
around, believes in your cult!
Angry expressions make one look like
     uncivilized & primitive.
In real terms, cost of losing one's
shirt are prohibitive.
Anger can be suppressed by thinking
of Him when nerves get a jolt.
Feeling is like that of a professional
horse-breeder when he beholds a
promising thorough-bred colt

Blowing hot & cold is an inconsistency
& inadequacy; great.
'Keeping cool' at all times, brings in
happiness & joy in its spate.
Remember, your anger won't effect
    this world's life style.
Except that, you would yourself
shorten your life by occasionally
    stirring up your bile.

* * *

A SWEET ENCOUNTER

I's lonely in the prime of my youth, until one day,
I felt vibrations compatible at first sight.
My boisterous, flamboyant thoughts flamed by vigor, youth and vitality,
abruptly stopped their flight.
Her mischievously parted lips held me spell bound and mind roving.
In her soothing eyes, I reckoned the rest of my life bright and promising.
My heart and mind helped each to say out
a polite and masculine offer with eyes conveying the rest.
Heart missed a beat at the mere thought of failure in the test.
Her magnanimous acceptance without any inquiry, sent ripples of ecstasy,
so profound, rich & deep although inexplicable, was my wild fantasy.
Blessed moment brought stability, reassurance and inner jubilation.
Blood gushed, life gleamed and body felt complete transformation.
Eyes saw and experienced pristine beauty in
His creation.
Our first encounter was a lifetime sensation.
Since then, life turned worth living and
kissing its 'ups and downs' with pleasure.
Now, my heart and soul started missing every
moment my life's treasure.
Life was restless when, I didn't see or talk to my love,
the whole world as if, just shrunk in my sweet and charming dove.
Mind always engaged in thought provoking exercises.
aimed to carve ways & means of giving her best.
Actions sometimes, I must admit, embarrassed world with my over zest.
Soon we united, breathing one breath with mind and soul majestically
intermingled.
With time flying, while our bodies twined, hearts pulsating blood for each
other, thoughts of ours kindled.

All I remember, is that the immense delight and pleasure
I derived from our first love collision, haven't experienced
that kind from any other Cosmic delusion.
We look at ours as symbols and replicas of
our sweet expression of pure love and mutual respect.
Each one reminds now and then sometimes a pinch of me
and sometimes a little bit of my sweet heart and of course our
Common debt.
Both of us now, through them, experience a Common flow of life.
For them, is enchantingly fascinating our strife.
We love and fight and fight to love day in and day out.
Together, we experience every now and then,
seeds of renewed love sprout.
Loving my heart throb is the only thought and act lovable.
Time will, no doubt, silence our physical love,
but can't make our souls inseparable.

* * *

LATE TIDES OF LOVE

Where were you all these years
when my springs were like autumn,
and my spirits perpetually at rock bottom?
Why didn't you encounter me some where sometime?
My youthful days, now gone with time,
leaving me only grey and sublime.
You had. wished to come why not then?
When, I drew spontaneous admiration from many
gallant and powerful men.
And the man in me, ever roaring like a fearful
lion at his den.
Your coming in my life, although very late,
has brought unfathomable pleasures in its spate.
Life now appears a tryst with destiny and fate.
Your nearness makes me feel unusually
rich that I care for no more wealth.
I adore the 'she' in you and her spiritual health.
It seems He made you for me and me, for just you.
A second of more life than otherwise destined,
in your company will do.
Since you have come, my passion is to see you smile.
When you do just that, my heart stops its rhythm a while.
But, then soon it restarts beating. pulsating stroke.
lest, darkness prevails on my eyes with over joy and I choke!
It was a struggle, it is, but every moment with
you, I, now enjoy.
A moment's separation from you makes me cry.
Love you, shall do so here and there-after.
Pleasure of loving you in this life than in uncertain many to come,
is worth a barter.

* * *

I LOVE YOU

I'm so lonely without you amidst so many,
like, a lady with her purse in a market, without a penny.
I see nothingness far and near,
what a waste, life is without you, oh! my dear?
My speech is without any vibration.
My actions incoherent as if a mere dictation.
My gait so dull and listless
like, without her master, a mistress.
My thoughts so superficial lacking depth and foresight
like, amidst stringed ones, a free kite.
My facial expression so pathetic as of deaf and dumb.
like, an archer without his thumb.
My apprehensions of life ahead, so weird
like, a callously clipped beard.
I look so restive and impatient
like a house-owner without his rent.
You're my only celebrity in life,
Without you,
I'm an unknown piece of an archive.
I'm unaware of dawn and dusk
like, musk deer without musk.
Without you, I'm just nobody.
Incomplete, like a soul separated from body.
Amidst the brightness of days,
I see blackness of dark nights.
like, a helpless pilot unable to prevent his
aircraft from losing heights.
Any kind of music fails to tickle my soul
like, an ace dribbler fumbling, when it's a sure shot goal.

Year, month, date and time are no longer my concern
like, a drug-addict's burnt up internal organs without a visible
burn
Liquor, no longer gives me any solace.
Like, a legendary sprinter's ignominy and indignation
after winning hands down a world class race.
My own images have become totally weird
and practically nostalgic.
Isn't my story tragic?
Please return me moments of my delight.
Since, living near my heart-throb's physical presence,
is my birth-right.
I seem to be living just for the sake of it.
Could I please live in my love's sweet
and benign nearness just a bit!

* * *

LOVE FORCE

I used to think love is a hoax.
Until I's neck deep in it.
I, now experience ecstasy and pain
never felt before,
it's an obvious case of total sell out
of heart and its core.
I remain engulfed in the envelope of her musk
Love is the only subject of inquiry and concern
from dawn to dusk.
My eyes ever search her near and far.
Body and soul, look upon her as Pointer Star.
In her nearness, I'm on top of the world
and restless without,
just like, pulled out of water, an angled trout.
Her pain spasms my entire body.
Her unhappiness makes me weary and tardy.
Roses and moon now, look dull and arouse
no more curiosity.
Even good eyes on her, engender my animosity.
My heart throb's sight, cools me and has effect of
sublime tranquility.
When out of sight, mind hovers on brinks of
savage brutality
Her angry words pierce and sound like notes of a wind mill.
Her misgivings cause utter confusion like, inside of an ant-hill.
I remain ever hungry of seeing her smile.
Charming sight beats the naked beauty of moonlight
on blue waters of river Nile.
I'm a living slave of my own choice;
ever ready to willingly receive her commands.

I bow in admiration to her wishes, tantrums
and even taunts.
Air around me is supercharged and I feel as if, galloping on my
white steed amidst world of ecstasy
and hilarious fun.
I now, fear none and am confident to tame incorrigible
ones without a gun.
Respect, envy, passion and tender compassions have all
come in its wake.
Her annoyance with me, makes me feel earth beneath shake.
When my eyes gaze into hers, I, see exquisite beauty
never seen before.
If surpasses magic charm of all the world's jungle and folk lore.
Moth loves fire and dives for death with an eternal kiss.
I'II go on waiting with hopeful note of my love without a hiss.
It true and honest love is God and God a truth; omnipresent,
shall seek Him through my love, is now my life's only challenge.

* * *

MY LOVE BOOK

You're the title and subject of my book of love.
Each page of which is smeared with sweet fragrance
of your enchanting musk,
Each word conveys my deep love; deeper than depths of ocean.
Going through it time and again, stirs up my
otherwise, stagnant life into motion.
Its appearance appeals right at the bottom of my heart.
I feel, it's like my own body part.
In every page, I, fathom smiling & charming face,
In this lonely life, it's possession is my only saving grace.
It's so personal that, I can't ask others to read.
Its physical nearness, seem to be my only need.
It's theme is my life-time encouragement.
Mere glancing through, provides life-long nourishment
I admit that the subject is too vast for me to do justice.
Each sentence is my passionate and emotionally surcharged
hug and kiss.
It requires no forewords and introductions since,
it's just an expression of benediction.
For me, it's invaluable and sacred
since, its gist is, the magic word of love without any hatred.

* * *

UNCENSORED SENSUOUS SEX

Just make sure you hold me tight.
Only at right places bite.
Go ahead & do me what you feel right
    all day and night.
Lead me for a perfect, blend.
Pure love denotes this trend.
Give me that pristine ecstasy & don't you offend.
I deserve all your warmth that you can lend.
I don't care whether you bend or mend.
Ensure your love holds me tight,
redress all past wrongs by doing everything just right.
Love me with tenderness & not just by brute might.
A passionate & aggressive try you might
Just make sure, end of your note is lovely & right.
Hold me tight.
Extinguish the fire in me all day and night.
Hold me tight.

* * *

I'M MORTALLY SCARED

If you love me, promise that
you'd give me company till
    I breathe my last.
Without you, I could wither
away and vanish from the scene rather fast.
Remember, our relationship
is that of ship deck and on it, it's mast.
In your nearness alone,
my present and future is promising like,
it was in the past.
That's why, our days of companionship have gone by so fast.
Fear of being left alone in my old days,
makes me feel dumb-struck and aghast.
Without you, in this vast ocean of humanity,
I could be all alone.
Mere thought chills and causes shiver in my very bone.
Besides you, who would be there to take care of this spent out cage?
Surely, it would be most
hopeless and helpless stage.
You've amply proven your indispensability for me time and time again.
Horrifying thoughts of
treading alone are my biggest bane.
I dread the very thought.
My imagination goes berserk and it causes in me a lot of
havoc and wrought.

* * *

LIFE IS A BIG WAIT

My journey from womb to tomb,
had been nothing but, a big wait.
At the end of the road, I don't
know if it's worth love or hate.
In mother's womb, I was waiting
impatiently, the day when, I,
    would be free to
      kick around with His grace.
Outside, as an infant, I always
waited to see out of all, only
      my mother's face.
I waited the day I could,
get on my own feet.
As a school urchin,
blessed moments, when my friend, I could meet.
As a senior school boy and collegiate,
I was seen waiting for my date.
As a young ardent lover,
anxiously awaiting for my mate.
Thereafter, sometimes for exam results or appointment letter or
    news of promotion.
or outside maternity wards, holding my breath,
waiting to hear our final results after that big commotion.
My desires to possess comfortable house and
possess best of everything made me work overtime; all in wait.
Awaited children's marriages,
their settling down and arrival of grand children
and great grand children till date.

I didn't know that my time was running out at such a fast rate.
Coming to think of it, now, all my life has gone by in its spate.
Now, I await moments when I'll call it a day.
Oh, I'm tired and sick of this agonizing wait to see at its climax,
Your benign divine ray.

* * *

COCKTAILS

DREAMY EXPECTATIONS

I'll sing for you the only dream I know;
We rode together through misty village way-side,
talked to each other's heart and there was nothing to hide.
We had differences and we had in common.
In nature's benign presence, as we galloped,
we left our differences behind,
Had nothing but love, just, love, in mind.
Our love was so peaceful and so blissful.
There was delight all around and life so meaningful.
We promised to share our sorrows and joys life-long.
Never shall we let our differences sink our spirits down.
As all good things come to an end,
a mighty storm rose and in its gushing dust,
I lost my partner at a road-bend.
I yelled and. cried and was stupefied at this cruel and rude shock.
Storm, Our ride, my beautiful partner now belonged to past.
I stood frozen and dead like a flag at half mast.
Shock was enough to startle me out of my sleep.
I closed my eyes desperately time and again to get back my dream.
Day in and day out, I live with sanguine hope & an acute desire;
to ride with my lovely partner yet in another dream.
Wonder, till then, will my spirits ever gleam!

* * *

BELIEVE YOU ME

When you laugh, the world laughs with you.
When you weep, you weep alone.
Known devil is better than the unknown.
An alive dog is better than a dead lion.
Don't think of buying castles with base coin..
It isn't good to change horses mid stream.
There are better ways to kill cat than choke her with cream.
Wanton kitten turns out to be a sober cat.
Head tends to get swollen up when it braves many a hat.
Sharper the storm, sooner it ends.
What you gain on roundabouts, you lose on bends.
A stitch in time saves nine.
There is no use throwing pearls before a swine.
Big sharks are busy gobbling up small shark.
All cats are grey in dark.
Two wrongs don't make one right.
Barking dogs seldom bite.
Higher a monkey climbs, more tail he shows.
One reaps only what one sows.
Fish stinks from head to tail.
For righteous cause, one has to fight tooth and nail.
Empty sack never stands upright.
Don't chose your wife and linen in candle light.
      Two heads are better than one.
Well begun is half done.
If a thing is to be done, it deserves to be done well.
Your actions alone decide your place in either heaven or hell.
Family that prays together, stays together.
Birds of same sort flock together.
After swallowing a cow, one can get choked on tail.

Rider can be lost for want of a nail.
Distant drums sound sweet.
Next to the bone is tender meat.
Truth lies at the bottom of the well.
Somewhere, in everyone's heart, the
innate goodness dwell.
         There is no use crying over spilt milk..
It's is wise to wear cotton if one can't afford silk.
Every dog has his day.
In a democracy, let even a donkey bray.
Strike when the iron is hot.
One who gets bulls eye, is the best shot.
One eyed is the king amongst blind.
Satisfaction and happiness belong to the mind.
Penniless man walks through the market fast.
He laughs longest who laughs last.
While in Rome, do as the Romans do.
It is wise to remain within one's shoe.
Empty vessels make more noise.
Everyone values one's uprightness and poise.
Many a good chicken have come out of tattered bags.
Toys can't keep busy old men and hags.
Old is gold.
Rich have their ice in summers and poor have it in biting cold.
There goes more in a marriage than four bare legs in the bed.
A liar's head is perpetually under a load of lead.
Dread of a sinner is worse than the sin.
In the ultimate analysis, no one is anyone's kith and kin.
Strange are the ways of God:
Remember, your pajamas stick on you
because of a simple knot on its chord.
Forthcoming events cast their shadows before.
For the one; suspicious by nature, there is no cure.
Hawks don't dive for the eye of another hawk.

It is futile waiting for skies to fall in order to catch a lark.
Beauty is a nine days wonder.
Clouds lacking depth only thunder.
Every dark cloud has a silver line.
Death of everyone has predestined place and time.
Wherever there is a will, there is a way.
Sincerity and honesty alone,
can turn your each day into a bright sunny day.
A deaf husband and a blind wife make a good pair.
Only courageous, upright and truthful dare.
Those, who live by sword, die by sword.
All that glitters is not gold.
Believe you me, you are all by yourself at the end of the road.
Time and tide don't wait.
To hook a fish, one has to use innocent looking bait.
Remember, only strength in character
Can make anyone's story great!

* * *

WITH YOU AND WITHOUT

I value your loyalty.
I cherish your identity.
I love your beauty within and without.
upon your physical charms, I get totally sold out.
You fascinate me all the times,
your benign nearness keeps me so sublime.
I adore your mental faculties.
When with you, I face no difficulties.
You please me with your simple and lovable nature.
Because of you, I have some stature.
Without you, I feel so lost.
For me, every moment of separation is at a
exorbitant cost.
My eyes seek you everywhere,
except you, nothing is worth a care.
For me, you're uniquely special and rare,
your painful separation, no longer, I can bear.
You are the only subject of my inquiry and dreams.
My very existence is due to you so it seems.
Loving you every moment is life-time pleasure.
'My love can't be. quantified by any measure.
Awaiting you, keeps me alive.
At the end of that agonizing wait,
my feet stir up as if, in a graceful Jive.'
Your lovable expressions of care for me drive me to hilt,
your sufferings without me, make me begin to wilt.
When with you, I get on to my high horse.

Without you, I get bucked and go for a toss.
Your mere touch alters my body chemistry.
In you, I keep adoring His artistry.
Without you, I'm like lemonade without lime.
I thank you profusely for being mine.

* * *

BODY RHYTHMS

Hi! do you hear the music of my love!
I'm sure you do, so let us dance.
Don't miss this chance.
When I hold, you'll experience both hot and cold
and I expect you to be bold,
when we dance,
so don't miss this chance.
I'll love you for it more than anyone could,
you deserve it so right from the bottom of my heart I would,
While we dance.
Don't miss this chance, let us dance.
I bet you'll enjoy,
you'll find me the right guy,
so, don't miss this chance, let us dance.
Baby, come on and have a dance.
My love will keep you in my arms even after drums go quiet,
I'll ensure my love is never out of sight;
After the dance,
So, don't miss this chance,
let us dance.

* * *

PARADOX

When you buy land, you buy stones.
When you buy meat, you buy bones.
When you buy roses, you buy thorns.
When you buy shoes, you buy corns.
When you buy cow, you buy horns.
Pleasures and sufferings are faces of the same coin.
One can't dismount when one rides a lion.
Rich have their ice in summers and
poor have it when air around is biting cold.
All that glitters, is not Gold.
Time and tide wait for no man.
Freshness and luster in skin comes after a tan.
To support one lie, one has to tell hundred lies.
In a game of Cricket, score goes up even with byes.
Adversity makes strange bed mates.
Even, reservoirs have flood water gates.
An ugly mole is termed a beauty spot.
Small pots get soon hot.
Beneath a source of light, it is dark.
Bigger Shark gobbles up a smaller Shark.
Maturity and wrinkle come with age.
Unfulfilled desires and hopes sprout anguish and rage:
Feeling of happiness and sorrow originate at the
same source.
Gain and loss of energy is enshrined in each force.
Money spinners generally, are themselves in a spin.
To keep things together, one has to prick a pin.
One has company yet, one is so alone.

All visible comforts have inherent latent groan.
One can take a horse to water source but, can't force him drink.
Any vessel could contain any liquid only up to its brim.
Whether right is might or might is right,
It is the breeze which, determines the direction in which to fly a kite.

* * *

FALSE AND TRUE MANIFESTATIONS

In lust,
dust dabbles, with dust without trust.
In pure love,
soul speaks through body.
Play isn't shoddy.
Lust is pseudo and transitory.
Love, truth and divine repository.
Lustful eyes conjure.
Love represents pure.
Lust play is just motions.
Love play, charged with emotions.
Lusty feign love and dramatize.
Love, tranquillize.
Lust is rude violence.
Love, bliss in silence.
Lust mirages heaps of pleasure.
Love, unlocks heavenly treasure.
Lust gives false kicks.
Love defies all tricks.
Lust is physical.
Love, meta-physic-spiritual.
Lust is mind imbalanced.
Love, a creative talent.
Lust aftermath renders pain.
Love, enfolds no shame.
Lust is reckless, hasty waste,
Love, denotes spiritual taste.
Lust is animal and savage instinct.
Love, a heavenly drink.

Lust is a brutal explosion.
Love, a perfect fusion.
Lust is tacit exploitation.
Love, an honest urge of exploration.
Lust vanishes in an ugly death.
Love, sprouts death after death.
Decide your choice.
Love, it's love, calls my inner voice.

* * *

RAIN SONG

Drip, drip, drip,
Parched earth beneath, tastes a heavenly sip.
Drip, drip, drip.
The spirit to oblige enshrined
in free floating cloud,
speaks volumes of humility and
graciousness of' Nature, benign.
Spontaneous, undisturbed, rhythmic flow
denotes grace, tranquility and wisdom sublime.
Drip, drip, drip.
Recipient sings an unusually alluring
thanks giving song.
Blissful uninterrupted down pour
is, as if, to redress a wrong.
Sun causes thirst and then let earth quench,
until she is completely drenched.
Drip, drip, drip.
Rain song is the sound of clapping
and ovation in Nature's award giving ceremony.
If you hear it in still dark night,
it's the purest symphony.
Drip, drip, drip.
It beats all man-made melodies and
tickles a deep rooted yearn for one's heart-throb.
In her absence, while witnessing
the nature's communion,
One's heart sighs and sob.
Drip, drip, drip.
Drip, drip, drip.

* * *

WITHOUT YOU, I AM

Like a,
House without wall.
Dead without pall.
Cuckoo without song.
Monastery without a monk.
Rose without a petal.
Road without it's metal.
Child without smile.
Egyptian culture without Nile.
Wine without punch.
Wafer without crunch.
Runner without spike.
Orator without a mike.
Music without tune.
Earth without moon.
Wire without charge.
Docks without a barge.
A school without teacher.
Ground without any feature.
Muscle without tissue.
Mother without an issue.
Mountain without a rock.
Bottle without a cork.
Canine without a bark.
Sky without a lark.
Winter without cold.
Ornaments without Gold.
A spider without web.
Dwindling spirits without any ebb.

A fair without Merry-Go-Round.
Musical strings without sound.
Pockets without money,
Beehive without honey.
Desert without camel.
Teeth without enamel.
Kingdom without a king.
Engagement without a ring.
Shoes without laces.
A track without races.
Birthday party without cake.
Mountains without a lake.
Cart without wheels.
Hamlet without fields.
Cycle without chain.
Town without a dame.
Tracks without a train.
Junkyard without a crane.
Man without brain.
Fields without grain:
Firing range without a shot.
Courtyard without a cot.
Body without life:
Old without his wife.
Tiger without his roar.
Culture without folk lore.
Aircraft without flier.
Shop keeper without a buyer.
Cricket match without a toss.
Business enterprise without a boss.
A doctor without stethoscope.
Cancer patient without a hope.

Reservoir without water.
Organization without any charter.
Study table without a chair.
Woman without her hair.
Child without any one's care.
Sandwich without a layer.
Military band without drum.
Bee without her hum.
Night without dream.
Milk without cream.
Boxer without spirits to fight.
City sky without a kite.
Calendar without a date.
Angler without bait,
Product without brand,
Landlord without land.
Woman without a fertile womb.
Grave without tomb.
Citizens without a right.
Metropolitan city without light.
Crown without a jewel.
Battlefield without a hand duel.
Battle front without rear.
Get together without a cheer.
Horse race without anxiety.
Worship without a deity.
A vase without a flower.
Observation post without a tower.
Kitchen without a cook,
    Library without a book..
Hunt without a hound.
City without a sound.
Canal without banks.
Battlefield without tanks.

Captive without a chain.
Love without suffering and pain.
Kite without a string.
Wasp without a sting.
Golfer without his cap.
Tourist without guide map.
Lock without key.
Hive without a bee.
Cycle without handle.
Married woman without a bangle.
Old city without a lane.
Hawker's market without bargain.
Merchant without a good.
Serpent without its hood.
Rugby without a fall.
Call girl without a call.
Tube light without choke.
Frog without a croak.
Shopkeeper without any sale.
Granny without a tale.
Virgin without her clothes.
USA without her highways & roads.
Underworld without crime.
Religion without a shrine.
Dog without turned up tail.
Hired criminal without bail.
Legendary story of tortoise without hare.
Owl without his stare.
Night without stars.
Casinos without bars.
Slot machine without tingling sound.
Hunter without a hound.
Bucket without a handle.
Candle stand without a candle.

Hospital without a doctor.
Picnic without a laughter.
Motor cyclist without crash helmet.
Curtains without a pelmet.
Jack & Jill without a pale.
Horse shoe without a nail.
Bow without arrow.
Bone without marrow.
Peacock without dance.
Cavalier without lance.
Boxers without referee.
Landscape without a tree.
Glow- worm without glow.
Brook without flow.
Man without moustache.
Cashier without cash.
Tribe without chief.
Tree without a leaf.
Battle field operation room without a map.
Town without a drinking water tap
Flower without a petal.
Kitchen without a kettle.
Rural India without a cart.
Rich without a big heart.
Cheeks without dimple.
Telephone without a tinkle.
Indian food without condiment
Mother without a sentiment
Rich lady without a maid
Snake-zoo without Crate
Dining table without a chair
Beauty pageant contestant without a hair
Dead without pyre
Soldier without fire

Brahmin without sacred thread.
Bakery without bread.
Greeks without tug of war.
Highway without a car.
Lion without den.
Writer without pen.
Hanger without its hook.
Hotel without a cook.
Ceiling fan without a regulator.
Jungle without a predator.
Pond without a lotus.
Microscope without focus.
Rhino without his horn.
Farmer without a corn.
Circus without trapeze.
'Pitza' without cheese.
Country without history.
Story without Mystery.
Well without water.
Clay without potter.
Mistress without her master.
Celebrations without laughter.
New born without his dad.
School without a lad.
Boxers without ring.
Soft drink without zing.
Rooster without call.
Football rivals without a ball.
Sea world without a shark.
City without a park.
Cemetery without an owl.
Beggar without a bowl.
Tree without fruit.
Para-jumper without chute.

Land without clouds.
Seed without sprout.
Elephant without tusk.
Deer without musk.
Cow without milk.
Sari store without silk.
Man without head
Sewing machine without thread.
Light machine gun without firer.
Taxi without a hirer.
Without you, life is a dead load.
I'm at the abrupt end of my road.

* * *

AGE AND YOU

If you are a woman;
At ten, she is like Asia; a great potential.
At 20, she is like Africa, half unexplored.
At 30, she is like India, warm, hospitable and worth visiting
At 40, she is like USA; technically superb.
At 50, she is like Latin America; Too good in kicking.
At 60, she is like Middle East; a great confusion and Mess.
At 70, she is like Antarctica; everyone knows where it is,
but, no one wants to be there.
If you are a man,
At 10, he is like a empty can.
At 20, very saucy and minty Ham.
At 30, quite crafty.
At 40, rather naughty.
At 50, tends to be fidgety.
At 60, finicky and catty.
At 70, ever ready to prove his dexterity.
At 80, always moving with a belt of chastity.
At 90, waiting silently & in his own style a celebrity.
If you are both man and woman,
Only rage increases with age.
Despite wishes, society does accept you as sage.
Whole life is like an unprinted book page.
Life regardless of age, is clap, clap and clap.
Analogous to a shaven head without a cap.
However, One blissfully doesn't know One's age,
i.e. the duration of captivity in this cage!

* * *

GOOD BYE MY LOVE

Hold my love, I've got my final call
It's His will and I can't let His life drama stall.
My body and mind remained loyal to you,
but what do I do with soul?
A free butterfly, now determined to leave my
corporate self cold.
- I'd been enormously rich with the wealth of your love
Wonder, I also, made you feel so!
But, now your impending separation makes me
feel awfully poor.
To retrieve my riches,
I'll continue to search you in my next attire for sure.
When I met you, it never occurred,
that one day I'll have to bid you good bye for good.
Even then, I couldn't
have pangs of anticipated separation withstood.
Even now, I feel the same warmth through
your touch that I ever felt,
the vivid, lurking fear in your mind has
already made my heart melt.
I thank you my love for bringing springs to my life.
Without thee, it would have been a veritable hell
and wasteful strife.
Your love made me do my part the way
He desired of me, most willingly.
Kiss me and help me now leave this world cheerfully.
Do wait, till I reappear hopefully, before it's too long.
Remember, I'm going to be always near you
humming my love song.

When the curtain draws, there is always ovation and applause.
My life is crying at my farewell, Aren't funny His laws?
Do close my eyes lest, I keep looking at you with
my butterfly gone.
Do bring my lips together lest, I keep singing our love song.
Life had been a bed of roses in your sweet nearness.
I fear no death now, under your warm breath and enchanting
caress.
Good-bye, take care, until I see you, hopefully, soon.
I'm incomplete without you like earth without her moon.
Remember, I'm withering only to love you in yet another form.
My soul, rest assured, until then, won't be calm.

* * *

LEST IT'S TOO LATE!

With every musky gust of spring morning breeze
across my face, I feel, as if, you kissed me.
With slipping waters under my feet of
receding tide, I feel, as if, my luck ditched me.
What do I do?
I'm a man with soft, tender and passionate heart,
how can I help it when only cruel separation
from my love is my lot!
What a life?
For half of it, went away without knowing your existence,
and the rest, in exasperating separated subsistence.
My body and soul need your scintillating touch.
You're an extra ordinary special one and I care for as much.
I am entangled in your love web,
like, an insect in a cob. web.
The trapped one puts up a life and death struggle to regain
freedom
I'm in it with my sweet will
and yearn to be in my love's kingdom.
Like, Spring is a source, it's water must flow,
and it's breeze must blow.
You're my source of life and-inspiration, & therefore, must let
me in your charming and glorious nearness grow.
Do you listen what I plead?
Your love is my only passion and greed.
Hurry up! and please hold my hand.
Lest, I go down beneath my, predestined piece of land!

* * *

MY WEAKNESS

You've no idea how much I love you
You've the foggiest idea, for
You, what do 1 do!
You think, I love you for your body.
Mere- thought to me, is naive and shoddy
I love you more than anyone could.
I'm sure, reciprocate my love you would.
It's the thee in you which keeps me enticed.
In your nearness, the 'I' in me. is missing and remains disguised.
My love is so strong that, it will impel
you to sing for me, love song.
My love is so benign that, it would see in you, no wrongs.
My love notes send out undying vibrations,
when you receive, strange enough,
you call them nightmares and hallucinations.
'I'm sure you don't mean it and aim to dodge.
I wait for you like a woman awaits for her soldier husband's
return from war.
For you, life long, my body sensory gates
will ever remain ajar.
So much of love would have moved any God of heavens by now!
I intend stirring passion and love in you
sometimes, wonder how?
If ever you see me,
Instantaneously you'd know how much
I love you,
and with that, your unfounded myth about me, shall blow.

* * *

PONDERABLE RHYMES

Your kind words, smiles, restraint on
temper and few good deed,
will make your enemies bleed.
Friends will unanimously wish you to lead.
Get to know how to think as well as What to think.
By service and love alone,
you can establish with Him a direct link.
Compassion, greed, lust and anger
suck you more and more into dark.
To quantify greatness, 'service before self'
is the only hall mark.
You're never alone as He's
always and everywhere with Thee
Turn your eyes inwards,
you're bound to see
Concentrate your
hearing faculties and you'll hear.
Thus, in meditation and trance, you'll find
Him more than near.
Dive deep into the depths of your heart
and you'll experience peace and solace.
Remember, success or failure will be known
only at the end of the race.
Law of cause and effect is inexorable,
unrelenting and universally rooted deep.
Keep in mind; whatever you sow,
so shall you obviously reap.

If you are peaceful, then alone,
you can radiate peace all around.
The joy that accrues due to selfless love,
devotion, sincerity and humility knows no bound.
Integrate your mental prowess's with
human compassion & emotion.
In being truthful to your conscience,
lies this lifetime riddle's, only solution.

* * *

TWO FACES OF THE SAME COIN

When I meet you, I feel it's been so long.
When I part, I feel our meeting went by
like a melodious song.
My whole life seems to be a big wait.
Yet, these autumns in my life, I don't hate.
As spring follows it close on its heel,
happiness and sorrow are part of my deal.
When I'm away, you're always in my mind.
Separation by itself, enshrines an enormous bind.
Days with you fly and without, make me cry.
Can't forget to think about you When,
I'm alone no matter, how hard, I try.
I wonder, if you too, feel the. same way!
Can't we have relation that of Sun and its ray
She goes away billions of mile
but, maintains a physical contact.
Their subsistence together
always and everywhere is a universal fact.
1 must confess too much of separation
causes in me stagnation.
However, separation and reunion to me,
seem to be my life's definition.

* * *

THINGS AROUND ME

Look at the curtain;
It'll go on hanging for you perhaps, till the pelmet gives in.
Look at yourself;
Your thoughts and deeds smack of only sin.
Look at the fan;
It'll go on comforting you without any sign of fatigue.
    Look at yourself;'
Under the aura of self created fears, lifelong you shriek.
Look at the mirror;
It reveals your impressions most truthful and pure
Look at yourself;
After wasting whole life, your mind, at fag end,
shamelessly seeks a spiritual cure.
Look at the bulb;
goes on glowing in order to remove darkness around.
Look at yourself;
Whole life you never treaded any truthful ground:
Look at the wall;
stands upright and for your protection, goes on bearing weight
    Look at yourself;..
You never tried to develop sincerely a spiritual taste.
Look. at this wire;
carries fire for you but, outwardly remains so cool.
Look at yourself;
Desires have enslaved your body and mind
and made you look like a fool.
Look at your shoes;
they love getting dirty in order to keep your feet clean.
Look at yourself;
Life long, you remained self centered and mean.

Look at this tap;
Gives you water regardless of time at your will.
Look at yourself;
You're ever ready to put over other's
genuine interests & rights on a sizzling grill.
When you shed tears, you shed a million ton load
just make sure, somehow,
that you don't do it at the end of the road.
The slogan of 'smiles, for others & tears for self,
for this volatile, turbulent and turmoiled
world society, perhaps, only could help!

* * *

HOW ABOUT A HELP!

Oh moon, Oh moon!
I'm tired and look upon you
as my last resort.
Look around and tell me where's my heart throb.
How's she, what has she worn and what's doing?
My sense of imagination is impaired and am incapable
of my heart wooing.
Beam on and check, if her mood is cheerful and full of glee,
or is she too morose, sad and depressed like me?
Tell her, my days are unusually long and nights'
unbearable & restless,
desperately, I await her response to my signals of distress.
Prompt her that I know not if I'm dead or alive.
Breathing seems purely mechanical now, to this hive.
Lament on my behalf that she didn't turn up on promised date,
consequently my whole life has turned out to be
an agonizing wait.
I don't feel thirsty and have no more urge for any food.
No delights. and pleasures of the world help alter my mood.
I 'keep toying with her and pretend to be inwardly glad.
The barbaric people ridicule me and think I'm mad.
I don't blame them as they, know not what love is.
No doubt it's painful, but, a heavenly bliss.
What's the matter, you too, are so quiet and sad?
Don't you know not helping the needy is rather bad?
I'm sure you are capable and have the will to help.
Do it please, do it before, 1 melt.

* * *

IT'S THE WAY YOU TAKE IT

Mother celebrates her son's birthday.
Father is sad thinking his death a year nearer now lay.
Unwed is terrified at her pregnancy.
The awareness tickles wedded couple's joy and fantasy.
An ardent lover sees his beloved in any young woman.
Heart-broken abhors the sight and calls it a bad omen.
We carry our wastes within us and consider self clean.
having shed, we don't want it to be seen.
A spoiled brat of rich parents looks upon studies a
waste of time.
A poor yearns for education and looks upon school as a
holy shrine.
Darkness and deserted places are horrid.
Both are welcome when, one is with one's beloved.
The sands of desert dance at the sight of a promising cloud.
Beach sands, at their sight, clamor for shroud.
When together, lovers find moon light exciting and
reverberating..
In separation, the same is painful and suffocating.
Monsoons bring cheers, jubilation and prosperity.
In its wake, floods, disease are obvious calamity.
Nothing is good or bad, it's thinking that makes it so.
Thoughts of what is good and what is bad in
varying situations, differently grow.

* * *

MY ETERNAL LOVE

For you, tell me where should I wait?
Give me one and just stick to that date.
Please ensure that you aren't late.
I would have bought a star beyond the ones that you see
That one will then, be exclusively for just you and me.
I would await sound of your steps on our promised land.
Keep waiting and longing to kiss the back of your hand.
Last time, you pointed towards this planet and I came.
Waited and wasted long years before you
lovingly called me by my name.
This episode is nothing but repetition of the same.
I have to go first to organize things for you so,
don't blame.
Don't delay your move please!
Loners around me there, will then tease.
You can't accompany me as
I've yet to decide where to settle down.
Also, before you come, I've to arrange my crown.
Don't you make me wait long,
lest, my throat go dry while singing our love song.
I promise, it's the last episode.
I'm sure you understand and will abide
by our perennial love code.
Will arrange your flight when you like.
Have you guided to our eternal dwelling
where, as usual, you'll see, from outside, our bike.
Don't you get engrossed after I leave,
with happenings of this world!
Here, there're false and pseudo illusions,
as many as could.

Your abode is, where I am,
and therefore, promise me to be there.
I know you would, as you are.
the only one, who cares.
I'm sure my sentiments and last wish you revere.
Come soon my love, so that, we could live forever.

* * *

THANKS GIVING

My temptations and aspirations are due to you as,
I love no one else.
My expressions and compassions are due to you as,
I adore no one else.
My strengths and weaknesses are due to you as,
I appreciate no one else.
My riches and poverty are due to you
as, my interests lie in no one else.
My passions and imaginations are due to you, as,
I find beautiful no one else.
My hopes and despairs are due to you,
       as, I'm charmed by no one else..
My moods of melancholy and jubilations are due to you,
as, I'm influenced by no one else.
My amusements, allurements are due to you,
as, I admire no one else.
My indulgences and juvenile delinquencies are due to you,
as, I like no one else.
My thoughts and dreams are due to you
as, in my heart, resides no one else.
Only your sublime and blissfully Charismatic effect,
helps me remain somewhat, sane.
That's why, for such a wonderful gift,
I thank Him profusely time and again.

* * *

HIS INVALUABLE GIFT

I'm one of those lucky ones,
gifted with perfect parentage.
The realization of this invaluable gift,
prompted me once to visit an orphanage.
With all my humility,
I brought sweets and toys as my humble gift
When I saw and talked to them,
my inner self got a jilt.
Parents of some,
had abandoned them and other's were no more.
All the same, they hadn't experienced the mother's
love which is universally solemn and pure.
Their eyes sought love and affections,
and their minds,
mother's protections,
They hadn't nestled with warmth
of their mother's breasts.
Obviously, had missed her cajoling, patting and sweet caress.
For them, words like Mamma and Papa were Greek.
No one got ruffled when they gave a shriek.
No one boasted when they learnt to walk
No one snapped them in children's park.
Nobody ever celebrated their birthday.
They were looked after on offerings
and by employees drawing regular pay.
When they beheld their agers throwing
to their mothers, a big tantrum,
they wondered why God had been so unjust to them!
Seeing them, I realized how lucky I'd been!
Analogous to this wonderful gift, I hadn't seen.

It's our moral duty to care for them, as they
behave like kids when, they get old.
Doing this duty, fetches many a comfort and pleasure,
so I'm told.
They lent you human form and nurtured with pure love
and affection.
Help them sail through trauma of old age with
utter satisfaction.

* * *

A LOVER'S SOB

You've given me so much,
wonder, will I ever be able to square up!
My existence without you, is a farce.
Lonely stretches painfully suffocating
and unbelievably harsh.
Hope of being with you somehow sustains.
Imprint of culture and civilization,
even in ruins, always remains.
Your touch alone, can vibrate, and resonate this instrument.
Other's would,
only be a sordid experiment.
Jasmine without it's fragrance, attracts nobody.
Cricket without umpire, would be so shoddy!
Breathing without you,
is merely mechanical and goes on.
All my senses keep awaiting arrival
of that promising dawn.
Your remembrance, though sweet yet, pains.
I'm virtually lost in a city
with innumerable crisscross lanes.
Where, there is no one to guide me to my destination.
My plight is like that of a patient needing
immediate resuscitation.
When will you come?
My moments of real celebrations and jubilation!
Remember, I'm willing to go with you to even hell
without any hesitation.

* * *

UNIQUE SIMILARITY

Expression of love in any language is sweet
and that of anger, crude and sour.
Whereas, time anywhere, is understood
in second, minute and hour.
All mother's concern for their children,
anywhere in the world, is incredibly alike.
Terrorists all over the world
possess exactly the same psyche.
Call of a child for mother, anywhere,
on our earth, is just the same.
There exists a great commonality
of meanings in different people's name.
Sky and stars from anywhere on
our earth, appear without any change.
Anywhere, one comes across
people exclaiming ways of
      God as strange.
Tears roll down the cheeks
all over the world, almost
in the same manner.
Amidst patriotic citizens of
different countries, there is
a unique similarity of
respect for their respective national banner.
Waterfalls, anywhere make
      exactly the same sound.
Hunters all over the world,
don't forget to take along for a
hunt, their hound.

Glow worm's sparkle anywhere
in the same way.
Dawn and dusk all over
are integral parts of any day.
Reverence for God, in the eyes
of a devotee of any religion,
    is uniquely similar.
A would be Hitler, anywhere would, need help of a
person like Himmlar.
There is a great commonality in every
aspect of life all over our globe.
In order to help mitigate man-made
differences, this subject is worth a probe.

* * *

WILD HORSES

Although, we live in absolute
wilderness, but in great harmony with nature.
Graze on wild pastures loving
and caring for one 'n' all of our clan
without craving for a high stature.
No one amongst us is a
King, and no one, his subject.
We have no particular attachment to
a piece of land or for that
     matter, any object.
We live together and run in one
direction in case of a common threat.
Whereas, man on flimsy grounds,
wastes his blood and sweat.
We wonder why, men can't
     live like we do!
Our wildness in wilderness
is thousand times better than
the civilized man in a
cosmopolitan city with his
     impeccable tie and shoe.
Concept of live and let live', you could, at least, learn
from us which, we amply display.
When you put the same in practice, you'll find
your days turning joyful and gay.

* * *

I'M IN SEARCH OF A BEACON

From the sea-shore, I watch
sea waters draped in darkness
    and silence.
Behind me, is land sleuthed in
blissful ignorance and savage
    violence.
There is fear of unknown ahead
and behind a dark and dismal
land with stinking dead.
Where do I go when I don't
see any ray of hope?
Also, all by myself, rigors of such merciless
environments how am I to cope?
In far distance, I reckon a flash of'
    beacon light,
there, too, I'm sure, environments won't change
at the bottom of that source at that height.
My hope lies only in emergence
    of moon;
Cool, quiet peaceful benign and for all of us,
    a rare boon.
I firmly believe that His message
would one day be understood by
all; beneath great waters and upon
    all land.
Rejuvenated & cheerfully, without any
anxiety and fears, I would then,
venture out in any direction and
turn my otherwise, tragic story,
    remarkably grand.

* * *

LITTLE THINGS GENERALLY GO UNNOTICED

I derive pleasure in watching:
Penguin's walk,
cat's stalk,
flight of a Dragon-fly
looks of a sly,
gait of a silk-worm,
Race motor-cyclist over a turn,
Fish jumping out of water,
anyone in fit of laughter,
Leopard's chase,
monkey in rage,
Tigress cuddling her cubs,
people's moods in city pubs,
a beehive grow,
jet shining blackness of a crow,
a spider netting web,
a toddler's first step,
looks of pet dog when in company
of his master,
A race horse at a crucial time
of race, getting faster,
Parrots and 'maenas' repeat their name,
match winning goal in
a world class soccer game.
leaps of a deer,
looks of a child who knows no fear,

A weaver bird weaving nest,
a school boy preparing for
    annual test.
A monkey, on orders, showing tricks.
An ass in joyful mood giving kicks.
In His beautiful creation,
this benign nature and other
forms of life are meant to
    be enjoyed,
and, certainly NOT meant to be destroyed.

* * *

WHOSE MISTAKE?

Life long, I craved for stars and moon
but, I got nothing except abject and
stark darkness of still night.
There was glimmer and brightness
all around but, I remained
in darkness right beneath a source of light.
Between moments of hope and despair,
I kept treading my pre-destined way.
That distant glimmer at the other
end of tunnel, kept me braving
the darkness through many a day.
I derived solace every now and then
when, I saw lesser forms somehow,
living without a moon.
Sight of four legged animals grazing
through thorns set my life's tone.
Now, I realize how my wants
had been the root cause of my
being in absolute dark.
I'd been like, on a fishing trawlers
deck, a tranquillized shark.
My story, I don't think, is grossly different
from that of any other.
That's like the realization of aircraft pilot
when his air machine is without a rudder.
Life, generally remains a mix of
good and bad like, a mixed fruit jam.
sometimes, one has to go empty stomach and
sometimes, it's a grand feast of ham, bread,
cheese and little lamb.

How I wish, I could perceive
the brightness of my dark nights!
How 1 wish, I could achieve
amidst, depths of materialism, my
spiritual heights!

* * *

MANAGE YOUR LOVE

Your love would put you through
    many a test.
You can't afford to lose your
    zeal and zest.
You've got to ensure that you
    do your best.
Then alone, you can hope to have
    real peace and rest.
When your love drives you crazy,
make sure your perceptions remain
    clear and don't go hazy.
Hard won love is more lovable.
Tough got love is more respectable.
Remember, she loves your
    man-hood and wit.
Take her out, look straight in
her eyes and hold her hand
lovingly when you beside her sit.
Let warmth and passions rise
    bit by bit.
Kindle in her love, fire and show
patience, till it's fully lit.
Let her be absolutely free and allow
her to take over when passions rise,
Be always fair and polite and don't
    you ever tell her lies.
Remember, if you aren't
    aching somewhere, you aren't doing it right.
Don't you stop till both of you
feel most relaxed and light.

After it's over, don't you for
God's sake, turn your back.
Knack of whispering soothing
words of admiration into her
ears, you mustn't lack.
Quality of your life depends
on how both of you live together.
Remember, only after temperance,
perseverance, patience and due
care, hide turns into a
    patent leather.
If you want accidents and bad stretches of life rare,
You have to, all throughout, take adequate care.

* * *

WISH I'RE!

I wish to be a bird;
free to fly whenever and wherever I feel like,
without inhibitions, fears, anxieties and
with absolutely trouble-free psyche.
I wish to be a jungle king;
free to move in which ever
direction I desire,
without hesitation and second
thought with zeal, swagger and great fire.
I wish to be as colorful as a peacock;
without fake colors and pretence and with
majestic aura around like a
monument out of one white marble rock.
I wish to be a mighty Banyan tree;
without creepers and parasites and with
air around absolutely fresh and free.
I wish to be amongst thorns a rose;
emitting fragrance without discrimination and
helping all to get into
joyful moods from tips to toes.
I wish to be any living being,
who could convey amply the
message of benign pristine nature.
Regardless of caste,
color, creed, religion, nation and social stature.

* * *

A PASSIONATE DESIRE

Blackness of night have now
    darkened my vision.
I've already lost my sense of
    accuracy and precision.
I yearn for you whole night.
At the end of it, my desperation
and frustration compels me
    to see nothing right.
Thunder and lightning, followed
by downpour add fuel to
    the fire.
I'm like a shopkeeper who,
for days together, doesn't
come across a buyer.
These lonely & painful nights
have blackened my heart
and mind as if, under the influence
    of black magic.
For how long am I expected to
stretch my life story, which is,
    most pathetically tragic!
Darkness of my nights have
    blocked my fate.
My very existence now, I hate.
was I to live my life
    engulfed and draped in
utter darkness of continuous black night?
To see my moon and live with it,
I think, is my justified birth right.

Without Thee, my life had
    been a big waste.
But, despite oppressive influence
of dark nights, I've
managed to stay somehow, sane and
chaste.
You're the only one who could
    bring in my dark life,
      some light.
Then alone, sky of my life, would be
    littered and dotted with
      all kinds of innumerable kite.
My wait is accompanied with
    deep sighs and moan
Come over and wipe my tears of
otherwise, dry eyes and help me
end my endless groan.

* * *

GOOD OLD DAYS

My yesteryears of marbles & kites
had days full of fun,
excitement & dreamy nights.
I know I'm not going to get them
    ever again.
This reality sometimes, makes me
    go berserk & insane.
Time went by playing street
    games without a worry.
I wonder why, did my good
    old days went by in such a hurry!
I's then a child & now
    I've children.
I's then, someone's grand
child & now I've grand children.
Why can't we now play around
those good old games?
Address each other by those same
old funny names?
Then, at the end of those peaceful nights,
my each day was, as if, with a new sun.
Life had no meaning or
    purpose but just fun.
whereas, now days are
marked with obligations, duty,
responsibilities & a feeling
as if, one was in a kind of
    never ending rat race.

Life, now, goes on at a slow
& very calculated pace.
Is there anyone who can
return me my childhood days;
whistling times of swings,
swivels & sways!
     My Good Old Days!

* * *

YOUR PROMISES KEPT ME GOING

Fire in me is extinguished now
    by my sighs & tear.
But still, you're nowhere near.
This agonizing wait
had dried up all charms &
    pleasures of my life.
That distant hope of seeing you
one day, kept me engaged with
    my wasteful strife.
If I'd known that my wait
    is going to be a never ending one,
I won't have showed up at
the start point of this
    wretched nerve-wrecking run.
My heart doesn't know the
art of beating, as my eyes
haven't yet seen the glimmer
    at the other end of tunnel,
How incomplete is a fuel sieve
when its without it's funnel?
My brain is nothing but a
    store house of fond remembrances
    & dreams,
overshadowing completely realism in
life, even at the end of the road, it seems.
I don't have to remind you
    solemn promises that you once made,
so distinctly & vividly, I remember
    till date.

Nothing is lost if, somehow,
you show up even on my last day.
Otherwise, for all my sufferings & privations,
you would alone be held accountable & shall
have to compensate & pay.

* * *

MUTUAL INDISPENSABILITY

Horn of vehicle is as important as perhaps it's brakes,
look and get up is as important as perhaps the cake,
warmth is as important as perhaps, the strength in grip of a
    hand shake,
environments are as important as perhaps, the spring.
Referee is as important as perhaps, the boxing ring.
Desert sand is as important as perhaps, the alluvial soil.
Serpent's hypnotic look is as important as perhaps, it's coil.
Revolutionary is as important as perhaps, a loyal.
A peasant is as important as perhaps, someone royal.
Similarly in man, courage is as important as perhaps,
    his politeness.
Fighting spirits are as important as perhaps, his calmness.
In this world, if you ever express or exhibit your fears,
rest assured, opportunists would make you cry and shed tears.

* * *

UNCENSORED DESIRE

Come over, I can't wait any more.
Life without you, is such a big bore.
I've never had such an urge before.
I swear, I love you from my heart's core.
So, come over and don't make me wait any more.
I desire your touch & want to feel you as much.
Don't disappoint and leave me in lurch.
Life without you, seem to have stopped as such.
So, come over and don't make me wait any more.
I long for your hold, come over lest, I go cold.
I want you to be bold.
So, come over as,
I can't wait any more.
My nights are longer than
days and days are dull & dreary without hopeful ray.
Each breath & moment is anything but gay.
So, come over and don't torment me any more.
My eyes with constant gaze have turned more than sore.
Come over and usher me into fantasy of pristine folk-lore.
Come over. Do you hear, as I just can't wait any more
live without you anymore.
Come over!
Come over!

* * *

MY LOVE IS FOR EVER

My love is blind and forever.
I'd be damned, if I, be clever.
Deep in the heart of that twilight zone,
my love tickles and thrills my very bone.
My love sounds as big as the other world.
Sweet and melodious as, notes of humming bird.
Loving you is more than fun on a beach.
Genuine professor's pleasure, when they teach.
No matter, I'm near or far, I'm, always on pig's back.
For my love's sake, I don't mind a sack.
My love makes me crazy.
It makes my visions sharp even when, it's misty and hazy.
It's a source of my only delight.
Sky divers' thrills at great heights.
It's primitive, aboriginal but, pure.
For all my ailments, the only cure.
It's continuation is my being's pristine rationale and belief.
for all my tensions, a safe & sure way to relief.

* * *

KID'S JOKER

In my town,
there's is a Clown.
His skin, dark-brown,
wears many a crown,
is generally seen marching
    up and down,
anywhere and everywhere in
    my town.
Blinks his eyes,
in the same breath. laughs and
    cries.
Makes-funny faces
while walking, ties his laces.
Leaving everyone amused,
walks away with deliberate paces.
He has no evil on mind.
In him, only entertainment &
    fun, people find.
His gestures are more than just
    kind.
Spontaneous laughter begets no
matter you see him from front
    or hind
His dress is more than funny,
rolls his tongue now and then
as if, tasting pure honey.
Entertains one-'n' all certainly
    not for money.

He is contented to see other
    happy.
jumps, chuckles and then pulls
    his nappy.
Thereafter, vanishes leaving
every one behind laughing his
    guts out.
Clown is certainly a better
person that most of us, no
    doubt!

* * *

TRUE IMPRESSIONS

I'm like a
trapped cloud in a deep valley,
helpless motorist in a car rally,
puzzled accountant whose, accounts don't tally,
face of someone, who has an empty belly,
pandemonium and confusion of an innocent, in a melee,
instability in a mass of jelly.
I'm a blend of
knowledge and ignorance,
funny whims and commonsense,
both at ease and tense,
sour and sweet.
coldness and heat,
bone and meat,
tradition and off-beat,
rationale and indiscreet,
a slope; both gentle and steep,
dear & cheap,
shallow & deep,
big and small.
short and tall,
anecdote amusing and pall,
mechanical robot and a hand-made doll,
spur and a knoll,
Rugby and ball,
day and night,
wrong and right,

depth and height,
black and white,
heavy and light,
weakness and might,
a tame and brave fight,
courage and fright,
I'm a judicious combination of both good and bad,
awareness of negative characteristics make me sometimes, sad.
Help me remove filth and dirt from my mind,
Just, once more towards me, be kind!

* * *

YOU WON'T FIND A MERCHANT LIKE ME

I'm a merchant of :
    moon-light,
    darkness of still night,
    sun's rays,
    future days,
    both faith & belief,
    happiness & grief.
Nature's fragrance & musk,
colors of dawn & dusk,
fascinating dream,
    life's steam.
    Smiles & cheers,
    laughter & tears,
    Rainbows of sky,
    pristine ecstasy, & sigh,
    toughness of mountains
    mist & musk of rains,
    blush of a maid,
    ambivalence in a shade,
    daring in a sacrifice,
    greed in game of Dice,
    whiteness of snow,
    spirit of arrow & bow,
    Depths of ocean
    energy behind any motion
Any & all of it, you could buy
from me at will.
Rest assured, you would get it
even if, your bank balance is nil.

* * *

TRUTH OF MY LIFE

When I see you, I lose control on my heart.
Thereafter, it behaves as if, it isn't my body's part.
You only, can tell whether it is foolish or innocent.
You only, can say whether it is being wise or gullible.
In your nearness, it makes my face
sometimes, pale and sometimes, aglow.
Makes my pace fast and sometimes,
unusually slow.
It doesn't believe that you're right there.
My face keeps on revealing
Inadvertently nervousness; mixed
with happiness thread-bare.
I can't be blamed for all my
acts as, my heart refuses all commands.
Simply, it turns down all my
civilized and legitimate demands.
When you go away, it behaves like as if mad.
Doesn't differentiate between good and bad
Makes me unusually morose and sad
I experience within, that vivid
transformation from a gentleman into a cad.
You, only can define my state,
I would accept your verdict
smilingly without a moan
& respect it without a groan.
Allow me to see you at all times.
That's the only way, I could
keep a check on my heart's record of crimes.

* * *

STRANGE UNIQUENESS

There is Unique beauty in a maid's blush,
a Unique urge in childhood
    to walk through slush.
There is Unique musk after
    first Monsoon shower,
a unique fragrance in
    mid night cactus flower.
There is unique strength in Unity,
a Unique sense of discretion in impunity.
There is a Unique kick in a perfect blend,
a Unique angularity and banking on a road bend.
There is a unique similarity in
    Mothers all over the world,
unique sameness in converting
    milk into curd.
There is a unique charm in doing anything in a
graceful manner
a unique fervor in upholding ones national banner.
There is a Unique sense of humanism in sharing
other's sufferings and own smiles.
A Unique wilderness in virile
    life -time memoirs.

* * *

I REMEMBER

In my early teens, one day, I,
was summoned by my dad.
He told me, in the world, nothing was
    good or bad.
Just watch out, deep love sometimes,
    drives one mad.
Life is worth a kiss
if you, ever get a worth while
    chance; don't miss.
In this show biz,
know well how to sell
    yourself and make hiss.
Don't trust anyone for his face,
don't step out without tying
    up your lace.
Be ever ready to work with your hands,
don't shy away from, venturing
out in distant lands.
Do everything right.
don't, for your legitimate right, ever
hesitate to fight.
Be on the lookout for graceful fun,
against a helpless, never
    pick up your gun.
Don't get unusually perturbed
when you get a cough.
Remember, life is short but
if you live it well and right,
    it's enough.

Your golden words now, I remember
    with reverence & thanks.
I've had, due to your advice.
huge deposits of love, affections,
enjoyment upon my life's banks.

* * *

CRAZY ME

To get a glimpse of your smile,
in a record-time
I pace up miles.
In a record breaking breath holding speed,
I bet you won't find someone of my creed.
Honestly, to keep you smiling
    is my only greed.
Beholding you smile, drives me crazy,
it's absence on your face makes me hazy.
Nothing is more important to me, than
    your bewitching smile.
The only way to euphoric
fanciful delinquency; juvenile.
I'm intrigued and bewildered
with your smile less face,
it doesn't remain for long and that's
the only saving grace.
Smile and keep smiling, I'll do
    anything for it.
So that, we keep knitting happily this
life together bit by bit.

* * *

EVER SINCE I'VE MET YOU

I seem to be on a merry-go-round,
I'm amidst heavenly sounds.
My heart so light,
stars at night are sparkling bright,
Smiles and cheers all around,
my ecstasy knows no bound.
Flowers seem to be giving their tender
    smiles.
Long distances appear only a few miles.
Air around me, gives me the requisite kick
I get happiness, one gets, on seeing
one's own house coming up brick by brick.
I get feeling of light -heartedness
even in linter
My life seem to be either on gallop
    or canter
Since then, I've open arms,
my heart dancing with times
    without qualms.
My mind open, clear and
    most optimistic.
My interactions with
    people, most healthy and hectic.
My feet always in beautiful
    steps of 'Jive.'
I'm since then, really alive.
Sky, now appears nearby and
    unusually blue.
Darling, only, ever since
I've met you!!

* * *

PROVE THY EXISTENCE

I'll believe in your existence if you
could;
wipe out poverty, hunger and ignorance
so that, there is end to all kinds of crimes,
human abuse and grievance.
Remove illiteracy and racial supremacy
so that, everyone may live with knowledge and amidst ecstasy.
Get rid of deviltry from human mind.
so that, everyone may turn gentle,
        benevolent and kind.
Leave no trace of human exploitation,
so that, everyone's future doesn't remain
        in a state of suspended animation.
Convert whatever is bad into good,
so that, everyone enjoys a great
religious fraternity and universal brotherhood.
Cut out earth-quakes, tornadoes,
volcanoes, epidemics and flood,
so that, such natural calamities and disasters,
don't cause loss of life and blood.
Turn our Earth's inside into minerals,
        jewels and black gold,
so that, children of poor countries, no
longer, suffer malnutrition, hunger and
        that biting cold.
Generate in every heart,
        acute awareness and respect for
        mother nature and'
        life in any form on our Globe.

So that, all of us, regardless
of caste, religion and creed,
untidily hand in hand help turn it into a heavenly abode.
Bestow upon all virtues of patience
  forbearance and temperance,
so that, all may respectfully address
each other with affectionate and fond
remembrance.
I bet, for you, it's an easy game.
I'd then really appreciate you and sing
Thy praises under any name.

* * *

SUCH IS MY LIFE

That unforgettable dawn of my
life brought with it a great
    festivity in air.
Musk and fragrance in a unique
blend; a phenomenon indeed rare.
Evening sky was littered with
    innumerable beautiful, kites.
As dark houses got lit up
with more colorful lights,
& sky was brilliant with
    countless glittering stars.
There were celebrations and cheers in
    city bars.
All this, I didn't care.
Since, in wait, my eyes gave
that hard and stony stare.
Until I was face to face with
    a dazzling glare.
Lo and behold, my beloved
    was there.
I didn't believe my eyes, so
    I, at once touched her.
My pent up emotions, then
    onwards, got a real stir.
Time in intense togetherness,
    flew, in unknown
    record time.

Another spell of loneliness;
such a harsh punishment for me, I wonder,
is a sequel to which crime?
So, I now, stare again in the
      emptiness of space,
renewed with optimism and hope.
In desperation sometimes, I
search, even that loose end of the rope.

* * *

PARADOXICAL HUMOUR IN REALISM

Ironically enough, I've seen
  Nain Singh, (one with eyes of a lion)
  a blind.
Buddhi Ram, (one with God's own intelligence)
  out of his mind
Daya Ram, (one with God's compassion and pity)
  most unkind.
Ganga & Gomti, (Two river names)
having bath under a city water tap.
Topiwala, (one who posseses caps) without a cap.
Sukh Chain Singh, (One like a happy and contented lion)
  without a nap.
Khushhal, (one who is prosperous)
  most miserable
Sundari, (Beautiful) most ugly and horrible.
Shoor Vir, (one who is brave in war)
  a coward and timid.
Suraj, (Sun) most cold and insipid.
Dhani Ram, (one who has God';s own wealth)
  like a beggar.
Ranjeet (victorious war hero) without
  a dagger
Shashi, (Moon) hot like sun.
Bandookwala, (one who possesses a gun)
  without a gun.
Man Mohan, (one who attracts every heart)
  an eye sore.
Santosh, (one with satisfaction)
  clamouring for more and more.

Shanti, (Synomymous of peace) full of
    anger and frustration.
Balwan, (one who posseses physical strength)
    most frail and weak.
Satish, (A symonym of Truth and God)
    a big liar and sneak.
Prem, (love) full of hatred.
Pavitra, (pure and sacred) any thing but sacred.
Vinod, (one who is always happy)
    without a smile and cheer.
Rondu mal (one who is always crying)
    without a tear.
Hoshiar Singh, (like an alert lion)
    a dud head.
Pawan kumar, (son of air) heavier
    than lead.
Subodh Kumar, (synonymous of education and intelligence)
    an illiterate.,
Jag Mohan, (one who is world's darling)
worth anyone's hate.
Shyam, (one who is dark in complexion)
    fairest of all.
Vishal, (one who is big and huge)
    anything but tall.
Basant, (Spring) most barren and dry.
Khushi Lal's (son of happiness)
plight, worth a pity and cry.
Despite odd examples above,
Indian names are so meaningful.
Their bearing and influence on
persons, so fascinating and beautiful!

* * *

PANGS OF SEPARATION

I'll do what you say,
    just do me a favor!
Somehow, cut short my separation and let me
experience once again my life's pleasure
    and flavor.
I'll sing whatever you desire if, you just
    oblige and come over.
Right now, I am pathetically unattractive
    like, a lawn without a mower.
I'll dance whenever you wish
    if, you end my agonizing wait.
That's the only way, I could live this life
with normal speed and gait.
I'll love you life long
    if you, somehow, appear before my eyes.
You may not be aware that I can no
longer heave any more painful sighs.
Waiting you for so long has turned me
    more than old.
Now, my body and mind are so well used
to sufferings that it really doesn't
matter whether it's hot or cold.
I can't brave pangs of separation anymore.
Life without you, is such a big bore.
Time now just hangs.
Heart in desperation and pain, most
Un rhythmically only bangs.

Blood somehow, is circulating my body
    without getting purified.
I get startled out of my sleep
    absolutely horrified.
Somehow, I am breathing as, there is
    a ray of hope.
Will I fall. short of my destination
when, I reach near, the top end of that invisible rope?

* * *

WHO AM I?

Day in and out, I ask self a simple question;
    who am I?
I have tried my best but till date, haven't found
the right answer, don't know why.
Simple it may seem, but it isn't so.
Unimportant and irrelevant it may appear, but it isn't one
    out of the row.
Because, it's correct answer will then, make you
ask yourself; so, what are you doing and what's your goal?
I presume, one can get to the right answer only after
one has most truthfully and honestly searched one's soul!
Have I come here only to drink, eat and dance?
or to keep a watch on incorrigible ones with
    my sword and lance?
Am I a sex machine always at work?
Or is it that my sole aim is to keep increasing my girth?
Have I come here to propagate irreligious things
    by being only superfluously religious?
Or is it that I have to pass through this way
    by being absolutely non-serious?
Am I here to pollute world's social and
    moral atmosphere?
Or am I going to top the list of big frauds,
debauches and hypocrites here?
Am I going to be an idealist and moralist only in thought?
Or is it that amidst abundance of water
I'm going to create conditions of drought?
Am I here to collect only gold?
And in its pursuit, keep causing aberrations
and deformities to my psyche mould?

Am I here to be a piece of amusement for
    all and sundry?
Or am I going to look neat and clean from outside alone
    like clothes from a laundry?
I certainly need better perceptions, knowledge
    and clear directions.
Only you, oh! my God, with your remote, could apply
    the required corrections!
    Who am I?

* * *

SPORADIC WHISTLING

I don't believe in tears.
Only, pray for one 'n' all's, smiles and cheers.
I don't wish bad for anyone.
Only, harmonious and deep humane relationship
      between all mothers sons
I don't want to see anyone without house,
      clothes and food.
Only, all living in peace and civility without
      being rude.
I don't crave for other's fortunes and riches.
Only, entire world society webbed to each other
      with invisible and unbreakable stitches.
I don't intend ever to make anyone sad and morose.
Only, one and all being charming and graceful from inside
and outside right up to their tips and toes.
I don't ask for my happiness and other's sorrow.
Only, for one and all a very bright and
      promising tomorrow.
I don't want to behold anyone suffer.
Only, all protected from natural calamities and
disasters by all time shock absorbing buffer.
If all think the way I do,
our earth will be inhabited by Gods from
      heaven too!

* * *

WHAT MORE COULD I ASK FOR?

Your very personal benign blessings were limitless
    at the time of my birth.
Otherwise, throughout my life, miseries and sufferings
wouldn't have found any dearth.
I was born to parents, who're young and full of life.
Without them, it wasn't possible to put up this world's strife.
Was born in perfect health with all body organs
    functioning absolutely normal.
My childhood was playful, joyful and so informal.
Brother, sister, relatives and friends made this journey
    so charming,
Without whom, it would have been so dull,
    boring and storming.
Without any privations, I got my life - partner;
    so beautiful and adorable.
Without whom, it would have been a mess; total and veritable.
I've. offspring's; beautiful and healthy.
Without whom, I wouldn't have called myself wealthy
I've heart and mind, which are sensibly
    sensitive and feel for poor and hapless.
Without which, there would have been no
difference between an animal and self,
I guess. due to my status, I live in honor and dignity.
Without which, there would have been no real peace and
serenity.
My intelligent sons, I am sure, would
    touch dizzy heights.
Without whom, my corporate remains won't
get well-deserved last rites.
Life seems meaningful and has a purpose.

Without which, there would have been no bounce and fuss.
I don't, in fact, see anything which, I don't possess.
I'm indeed grateful to You beyond words
    for Your personal, kind cares and caress.
I plead Thee to ensure that when,
I call it a day, I'm dependent on none.
I should go away smiling and
thanking You for all that You have, for me so graciously done!

* * *

TIME ONCE GONE, IS LOST FOR EVER

My heart beats only for you.
Anything you ask, I'll do.
I'm sure, one day, you'd reciprocate too!
I don't think you know me well.
That's why, I'm getting hell.
Reason one day, you've to tell.
Right or Wrong,
I must continue my love song.
You ought to come over before it's too long.
My inner rhythm is getting dilated,
on minor things, I get grated
because, my well deserved pleasures are
        getting pirated.
I don't know whom to blame!
Times will never be the same.
You must know that right now, I'm
        like a lamp without flame.
Nothing turns me on &
nothing thrills my bone,
everything that I ever possessed, seems gone.
It's high time, you come around.
My 'Think tank' seems to have run aground
impatiently, \I await your foot-step's sound.
We'll never get this time again.
It gets lost like a child on junction of
        many a lane.
Soon, it'll all be quiet like immediately
        after a big rain.
Only your presence can bring me a smile.
Help me get it just once, for a while.

For that, I'm willing to change my
    rhythm & style.
So, come over without any more wait.
otherwise, I'll soon be emotionless at
    this rate,
and then, whole world I'd hate
I'm sure you don't want that,
so, help bell the cat.
In your honor, I'm awaiting to bow
    and take off my hat

* * *

I HATE SOME

My hatred,
to me, is rather sacred.
I hate liars,
human flesh sellers and buyers.
I detest those, who hit below the belt,
those, who, on other's sufferings,
    deceitfully pose to melt,
I abhor the sight of shop-keepers
    in service uniforms.
those who, cause in innocent's lives
    tempests and storms.
I deplore all with double face,
all those who, cheat others throughout
    their life-race.
I hate religious teachers who, preach
    dastardly crimes against followers
    of other faith.
All those who take arbitrary decisions
    on vital national issues in a
    great haste.
I decry nefarious activities of all
    disloyal,
all those who, on other's toil lead
    a life, regal and royal.
I abhor the sight of anti national
    in all form,
all those who, breach peace and
    established norm.

I detest those who, twist law-abiding
    citizen's arm,
all those who, cause country's name
    and reputation, any harm.
I hate Government servants who belie
    people's trust,
all those who, get jealous when in
neighbor's house, crackers of happiness
    and celebrations burst.
I hate these men for the sake of my nation.
All should, the same way, without any
    hesitation!

* * *

STRAY THOUGHTS

Life is, what time unfolds.
Measure of riches is, what one inside holds.
When you stare in mirror, it reveals your
    true-self thread bare.
Advancement of any society is fathomed by how
much aged, children and women get care.
Living from one breath to another, is ground reality.
Hatred is that evil source which, sprouts savage brutality.
As hunger is the best sauce,
loss of moral courage is the worst loss.
There is no point dying number of times each day,
how can you hope to see at the end of the
    road that Divine ray?
It may be easy to hoodwink others for some,
you may repent your speech but certainly you
won't if you use discretion and keep mum.
Love of life is justified as long as one
    respects other's right to live.
Greatness can only be identified by how much
to others, you give.
Beautiful is only that, who, has inside real beauty.
Only that country is great, whose citizens are
conscientiously alive to their duty.
No hair dyes and henna can make anyone young.
There can't be more potent a weapon than tongue.
That country can't blossom whose children
    don't have dreams.
Physical beauty is a nine days wonder, so to me,
    it seems.

His glorious divine light glows in all religion
    shrines.
If one reads in between the lines.
"All religious books convey
universal brotherhood as a common message
Remember, preachings of Ram, Rahim, Christ &
Nanak are our common heritage.

* * *

WHAT A WASTE?

One third of my prime life went by
without knowing your existence
and then, one third in tears,
because of our physical separation.
Uncertain prospects of last one third,
now tickle my wild imagination.
Then, I would be old and spent,
my physical powers retarded and body bent,
with teeth gone, knees buckling
and eyes shy of day light,
how would I care, love you and more importantly fight?
How would I hear the sounds of
your foot-steps when my ears
would refuse to hear a near bang?
How would I look after you
when time upon me would just hang?
I hear, in old age, love gets deeper.
Old ones stick to each other like, any
tree and upon it, a creeper.
Still, I look forward to that last
One third as, at least, I'm
assured of your charming company.
I would like you to be care-taker
of all my riches and money.
Thereafter, soon you would get my call,
meanwhile, rest assured, I'd have
arranged with Him to live
with you uninterrupted my love, right from the start.

* * *

ELIXIR OF MY LIFE

You've made it for me, a
    charming and meaningful life.
You're His unique gift to
    me in the form of my wife.
Without you, it'd have been
    so dark, dismal and utter confusion
So boring, jarring and a
    great illusion!
Anywhere, I see you,
    hear & feel your
love and caress,
somehow, I'm confident
I would face squarely, this world's
    stress and duress.
I don't know what good in
    me you see!
I'm a mixture of both good and bad
deeply enshrined in any human that be.
I need you more than ever now.
With courtesy and humility, as
thanks giving to you, I must,
    life long, bow.
Your continued
companionship, I need even
here after.

With that promise and assurance, I would
kiss death with cheers and
    thousand laughter.
You give me that requisite
    inspiration and motivation to go on.
When will I behold you my love?
Impatiently, I await light of that dawn!

* * *

BEAUTIFUL RELATIONSHIP

Like honey-bee needs a flower,
lighthouse needs a tower,
moon lit-night needs a moon,
day warmth needs a noon,
love needs someone worth loving,
lawn grass needs mower for mowing,
Jockey needs a thorough bred colt,
lethargic needs a jolt,
Any organization, needs a boss,
High fidelity music needs perfect bass,
life needs a breath,
soul for rebirth, needs body's death,
flute needs lips,
For divine pleasures, soul needs
      heavenly dips.
For friendship, one needs a friend,
fashion in vogue needs a trend,
patient needs a doctor,
tank buster in modern battlefield needs a potent
      heli - copter
Life on earth, needs perfect ecology,
civilization needs mythology,
company manager needs someone
      to take down dictation.
National flag needs existence and recognition of
a sovereign nation.
Life needs hope
Orator, to hold his audience, needs
      that invisible rope.
Shop -keeper needs customer,

Military band needs a drummer,
pleader needs clients,
Children stories need giants,
deep love needs sighs of separation,
Infertile & parched lands need inundation.
Similarly, everyone in this
world needs love.
No matter, whether under water, beneath
    ground or above.
Therefore, don't hesitate and give despite inhibitions,
    as much as you can.,
Remember, fair skin for a real glow, needs a tan.

* * *

HEART TO HEART TALK

Two hearts in two different bodies beating
    synchronous beat,
energizing for each other required warmth & heat.
Pumping blood as if, for each other.
Expressing happiness on their wonderful relationship
like infant baby does at the sight of her mother.
Talking to each other silently despite distances,
feeling compassionately for each other despite cosmic
    hindrances.
One day, one said to other, "why don't you
rest while; I would work on your behalf?"
The other on hearing it, had a big laugh.
"If I stop, you silly," said the other, "How
would I, when I want to, come back to life?
"My body along with me by then, would have been given the last
right!"
"Sensible" said the first one, "But, make sure &
promise that you won't stop before I do"
"Yah! said the other "that's a fair deal otherwise,
I'll absolutely be lost without you"
Let us also take a vow that we won't break
each other's heart as, in each cage, there is just one.
"We'll go on loving each other & hurt none."
Bless us that all of us have such warm,
    compassionate & lovable hearts
Then alone, this world caravan perhaps,
despite apparent differences,
could keep together
    all its Carts!

* * *

I CAN'T HELP IT

This dark, misty, musky & wet night
 kindles in me a deep urge.
Emotions, sentiments, passions, presentiments
& desire in a unique blend within me, merge.
I await silently sounds of your foot-steps,
my eyes constantly gaze through the door to
 get your glimpse from the farthest.
Lightening, thunder & rain make me more sensuous.
Love calls of Frogs & Toads make me more anxious.
To seek touch of my love, in such a charming night,
is my birth right.
You must know that by now your
photograph is a poor substitute
These moments of our separation without
respite, most nostalgically, haunt & hoot.
I'm sure sometime, moon will show up
 while, it's still dark.
With Its halo through thin clouds, leave
 on me, an indelible mark.
No one else except you, my love, is my moon
 that I, impatiently await.
You must know I'm desperately looking forward
 to behold your charming gait.
I'm sure you would listen to my inner yearn
& not let me, in this wet night, any more, burn!
 If you don't make it, you'd find my.
 eyes stoned & still.
Your Continued absence & my stirred up
emotions, by first light, would cause
 a sure kill.
 I can't help it!

* * *

INDIAN COSMOPOLITAN CITY

On roads, rows of Cars & Cars,
In pubs, Whisky glasses & jars.
Glittering & decorated shops & shops,
no sight of any fields & crops.
Hoards of people busy like bee,
most faces lifeless, grim without glee.
In peak office hours, everyone in a great rush,
many places where affairs are conducted in a
    great hush.
Everyone seems in a great hurry as if,
    members of a fire brigade,
Kidnappers, pick-pockets, boot legers &
smack- peddlers, ever spreading their tirade.
Air pollution beyond human tolerance,
water contamination more than significant.
Heaps & mounds of rubbish & refuge around.
Schools running amidst deafening city sounds.
Big market centers where, money seems to be in no dearth,
restaurants & way - side fast food joints.
    with ever swelling girth.
Bus alleys jam-packed & people hanging out side.
People seen going & coming every where
    as if, waves of a high-tide.
A few parks and play grounds,
a great noise - pollution due to host of sounds.
Cops busy in controlling traffic and crowds,
vehicle horns & hawker's calling more than loud.

Sky - scrapers kissing skies,
over slum-dwellers sighs & cries.,
Fashion in exuberance,
Crime in abundance,
Night clubs, discotheques Red-light joints,
more than busy
life in general both still & fizzy
Naked exhibitions of road-rage
markets full of both sexes of diverse age.
Life, in general, incredibly fast & dictated as if,
by a remote,
where many a beggar would tender even
    a hundred rupee note.
Extravaganza of variety of lights at night,
Interaction of multi- rich, rich, middle men &
        poor at sight.
Indian cosmopolitan city is a life time experience,
a hard test, for a typical villager's nerves & forbearance.

* * *

CAN I DO ANYTHING
EXCEPT BOW TO HIS WILL?

With them are gone days of
Seeing my young ones awaiting and
greeting with beaks wide ajar.
Sight of their tumbling out of egg
shell without a scar.
Days of our nest weaving with love and care.
It's bed strewn with soft petal
cushions layer after layer.
Moments of desperate search for best of insects & fruits.
And, holding them close to chest under
wings, on hearing wild owl's hoots.
Days of imparting lessons of hops & flight.
And, how to live through arduous and scary night.
One never imagined ever, that once,
they're on their own, they'd leave for good.
His mysterious ways, I've never understood.
I's alone and now, alone once again.
I won't know if my past was a dead loss or of some gain?
I must now, abandon my nest.
Go out and face again the rigors
of outside world with same fervor and zest.
There is a lot of wisdom in good
old saying 'What can't be cured, must be endured.'
Otherwise, sufferings of life would
Make it rather tardy, nerve- wrecking & a big bore.

* * *

AN EASY WAY

Everyone seems to be busy with his life,
fixes goals & hence strife.
Finds time to be at premium & hence
    runs around.
Everywhere, he is just watch - bound.
All his efforts & results please only his body & mind.
He's completely forgotten about his soul &
    left it somewhere far behind.
Heart, soul & mind have to be integrated for overall best results &
also, in order to avoid failures & insults.
Soul i.e. inner voice is equally, if not more important than all.
Like, in any game of bat in any form, a ball.
Progress on both fronts i.e. materialism, & spiritualism
can go on side by side.
Heart & mind then, keep on reinforcing each other
    with trust & faith between them,
    without anything to hide.
Life, will go on without a pause till, the very
    last.
Irony is, everyone gets surprised as to how
    it all, finished off so fast!

* * *

PSEUDO & WASTEFUL EFFORTS

People visit temples & mosques to be with Him,
not realizing that, He resides all the time within.
People visit shrines to get His personal care,
not realizing that, by listening to own conscience,
thoughts on all subjects, directly with Him, they
    could share.
People, in order to find the right path, pay visits
    to monks & preachers,
not realizing that, inner voices on all subjects are
    the best teachers.
People follow meaningless religious customs, dogmas,
    rituals & ceremonies aimed to
    placate Him,
not realizing that, all these are a big waste of money &
time & through these, prospects of achieving anything
    meaningful, are absolutely dim.
Some pose to be close to Him & appear to the
    world, as saints & sages.,
People visit them to pay their respects'& worldly offerings,
not realizing that, false exhibitions on their part,
    are a mere, any teacher's & swindler's dramatic stages:
If you want to live with Him,
    there's no need to go or do anything anywhere.
Just dive deep into inner depths & feel &
fathom His personal existence in His true form, thread bare.

* * *

WAY TO SUCCESS

Act fearlessly.
Argue logically.
Behave nicely.
Communicate clearly.
Dress smartly
Earn honestly.
Give generously.
Handle tactfully.
Judge impartially.
Manage appropriately.
Pay promptly.
Risk cautiously.
Spend intelligently.
Think constructively.
Serve willingly.
Invest prudently.
Listen attentively.
Observe curiously.
Admonish privately.
Reward publicly.
Question cleverly.
Read selectively.
Tell briefly.
Work efficiently.
The bottom line is, for meaningful success,
sincerity of thought & purpose is a must.,
Remember, first is always first!

* * *

COMMON REALISATION

I'm amidst materialistic whirlpools and quick sands.
I need for sure expert helping hands.
Without them, there seems no hope,
spiritless, I'm destined to continue to grope.
I journeyed through the heart of darkness ever
and throughout, I thought myself to be unusually clever.
At the end of it, I now realize the kind of mess I'm in.
Towards my soul, I've committed sin after sin
It would have been blissful, had 1 followed 'simple living and
high thinking' course,
It would have been possible then, to have remained always
close to my source.
At the moment, there is so much of separation that 1 don't
think, it's possible to cover this wide gap.
As, there is no time left between now and my eternal nap.
When I glance through the pages of my life, I find nothing
meaningful and of any interest.
How I wish I'd known it at the very outset!
I'm left with no alternative but to say next time.
I wonder would He afford me yet another chance & be kind!
All of us fathom the realities of life rather late,
because the illusions & delusions of this
materialistic world around us, have many a enticing bait.

* * *

YOU CAN CALL SHOTS

When one loses the basic will to live,
rest assured, thereafter, for this world, one is left with nothing to give.
People experience that because of total disenchantment,
realizing the realities of life with disillusionment.
Therefore, the number of remaining breaths is any one's guess.
In fact, some await impatiently the blessed
time which is to put an end to this veritable mess.
Life goes on as long as there is will.
Like, without breeze the wind mill would be still.
Some say at the time of retirement from their job, that they are
sick of work & need rest,
and only attend to mundane house-hold chores or attend to
garden at best.
Soon, they realize that they run out of their zest.
Time then hangs on,
moments turn out to be years & somehow usher in
yet another stereotyped dawn.
Thus, one is bound to leave this world in misery.
As, before finally putting down-shutters, mind flashes back all
weird images of the sordid life history.
Life regardless of its span, is worth it if, it's with a noble
    purpose or aim.
Without which, all your excuses to justify your life events
    are more than lame.
A noble cause will keep you energized with a will to go on.
At the end of it, there would be happiness, smiles,
cheers, celebrations & jubilations, so forth & so on.

* * *

CLEAN YOURSELF BY EACH BREATH

Time, place & person has a great interrelation;
Where ever, all three get together, person
leaves for his next destination.
All three are fixed & pre-ordained.
There is nothing what-so-ever with the help of which the same
could be proponed or postponed..
Wash yourself from inside with the soap of Recitation
of His name with each breath,
throughout life's length & breadth.
Use perfumes of actions that He dictates
Then, the musk & fragrance around you
would leave mesmerized even the most
        poisonous of crates.
With that, your face would glow &
        radiate like the great sun.
Then, on whom so ever, you cast a glance, the
demon in him would get tamed without a gun
wherever you look at,
You'll spell innate peace; sublime
and help destroy the demon in others
        who's, ever ready to commit a crime
Life is really a very short spell
It's here you decide for yourself
        the place in heaven or hell.
Clean yourself from inside as
early a stage as you can,
& then, be worthy of being addressed
by Him as His own man.

In communion with God,. recitation
of His name would produce such beautiful sound
which, would cause real peace in &
    around.
People give bath after you've gone
whereas, life-long from inside, you
remained dirty and stinking
like a deceitful monk.
You could easily do it if, you have the will.
That's the way the demon &satanic spirits,
    you could kill.

* * *

FRIENDSHIP

They say 'a friend in need is a friend indeed'
and I say 'a true friend is one, who is friendly
both in thought and deed'.
To have a friend one has to be one.
For brightness, there has to be a visible sun.
A genuine friend would, both happiness & grief, share
and in these days are indeed very rare.
A friend you could find in anyone regardless of sex & age,
perhaps at any life's stage.
A good friend helps stabilize turbulent heart & mind.
helps set life's cruise on peaceful ways
leaving sordid past behind.
A sincere & honest friend is His one of worldly
ways of getting close
and making one sip a heavenly doze.
Those who have genuine friend's company,
find their life span as a very pleasant journey.
Yet, there's a friend always within,
whose friendship would keep you far away from all kinds of sin.
He is there with you day & height to listen your woes & sighs.
To be with Him, you've to just call for Him after
closing your eyes.
Try Him once & give Him a genuine try.
I'm sure, it would put an end to all your Him
anxieties, fears, stress &cry!

* * *

I MISS YOU

Your life spark adorned the garb that I have and,
you gave me a name.
Your physical, mental, spiritual and metaphysical traits
right from inception, in my conscience, came.
You reared me up as, I was only your extension.
Sight of my suffering in any form;
was moments of your agony and tension.
I's on top of the world, when I, held your little finger
and ventured to see this world fair.
I got on to my feet and learnt to walk
under your personal and benign care.
As long as you're there, I had no fears.
Life was full of cheers and my cheeks never tasted
the salt of my tears.
You gave up your comforts for my pleasure.
In fact, to quantify your sacrifices for me,
I've no measure.
Without you, I'm like a Child in a fair;
without the touch of his Dad's little finger.
Memories of your sweet caress and my looking
into the world behind, from over your shoulders,
in my conscience always linger.
In you, besides a father, I've lost a genuine
friend, philosopher and guide.
With this mortal blow, I find none else by my side.
You've left behind on grain of my mind,
indelible foot prints of all size,
painted with bewitching sky-colors of sun set and rise.
Your passing away is a grim reminder of a fact
that, now, it's my turn.

Similarly one day, if I'm lucky, my sons too,
would make me burn.
I feel you're very much present in me and alive.
I must tread on the path shown by you and sincerely strive.
To see your dreams come true through me,
to my mind, will be my real tribute.
To your sublime humanism, humility and humor in me,
    I solemnly salute..
I miss you.

* * *

FOOTNOTES:

1   Cult of non violence
2   A saint who practices doing duty unmindful of returns
3   Hindu's most sacred book.
4   Sect of Hindus who were to live & die for the protection of the Hindu society as warriors
5   A Concept of Utopian Kingdom.
6   Gangotri glacier (source of Ganges) is geologically inter Connected with great Man Sarover lake area in Tibbet.
7   Days of festivity in Assam
8   Bodo folk song.
9   Mishing folk dance
10   Tiwas folk festival.
11   One major crop over the year
12   A state of freedom for soul when it doesn't take rebirth.
13   Religious priest who conducts last rites
14   Present time period of approximately 27600 years in Hindu mythology. Three such time periods of human civilizations are over & now it is the fourth & this is the last one which, will end in complete annihilation of all life on the earth.
15   Act as per duty & moral responsibility regardless of returns
16   Hindu's religious book.